D0531734

THE
AIREDALE TERRIER
TODAY

Janet Huxley

Howell Book House

New York

HOWELL BOOK HOUSE
IDG Books Worldwide, Inc.
909 Third Avenue
New York, NY10022

ISBN 0-76456-109-X

Library of Congress Cataloging-in-Publication Data
available on request

Manufactured in Singapore

10 9 8 7 6 5 4 3 2 1

ACKNOWLEDGEMENTS

To my dear 'Big T', for the love, patience and thoughtfulness with which you have showered me and for the humour and friendship from my daughters, Dawn and Julie, who understood how time-consuming this project has been. I also thank my loving sons-in-law, John and David.

To my darling grand-daughters, Emily and Nicole, two of my 'special baby Gems', whose photographs are in the Pet Airedale book. Your great-grandma Mary (my Mum) was a rock as usual; she served all of us pop and tea on that hot and sunny day while Stephanie's camera was clicking.

To Dad (Merlin): it is a smashing photo of you cuddling the 'agility' Airedale of Muriel's.

To Aaron, the third 'special baby Gem' and my youngest grandson – sorry, but you were only a babe in arms; not sure, now you're in junior class and sixteen months old, whether you would have cuddled the dogs or tried to knock 'em out!

There are so many people whose kindness I shall never be able to repay. I have honestly tried to depict as many Airedales and owners of the breed as was possible – not an easy task. For those who are not included, my humble apologies, and, for any problems, see Big T! To mention each person individually would occupy a chapter, and so I will have to name but a few.

The highly respected Ekatepuha Cehaweliko (Ekaterina Senashenko), Expert of the RCF (Russian Canine Federation), has kindly written about the history of Russia's Airedales. This was translated especially for me by my friends Tatiana A. Shurigina and Slava V. Kovalsky in Vladivostok. I also thank Galina Rudenkova from Yoshkar-Ola for her article on current exhibitors in Russia and Margaret Saltzmann (Hugadale), a long-standing friend from Ontario, for her help with Canada. My thanks to Mareth Kipp who covered the USA.

Andrew Brace (Tragband) must be mentioned for his humour, encouragement and enlightened thoughts about judging. I am indebted to the renowned Airedale artist Annie Curran (Ragtail), who contributed her beautiful line drawings, to Danny Gilmour (Dumbriton) for his genetic knowledge and teachings, and to the experts for their insight into breeding programmes. All those who have contributed their time freely are mentioned in individual sections.

To all my friends and associates – I shall never forget your kindness.

Janet Huxley

CONTENTS

1 ORIGINS AND HISTORY OF THE AIREDALE TERRIER

Many Yorkshire people take pride in the fact that the Airedale Terrier originated in their county and, by travelling back in time, we can discover how the Airedale saw the light of day as one of the native canine breeds of Great Britain.

As the Industrial Revolution progressed during the 1800s, the area around Leeds and Bradford was full of mills emitting smoke from their tall chimneys, coal mines with their shaft wheels turning, and factories sounding the day's ending with their sirens. The workers, in what little leisure time they had, centred their interests on the River Aire, because part of its course runs through those towns.

The animals found in the Aire valley provided endless hours of sport, so terriers were bred to work and hunt otters, water rats, polecats, martens, weasels, rabbits, hares, badgers, ducks and moorhens. These pursuits could also prove profitable for the sporting workers, because side bets took take place at the so-called 'Water Rat' matches.

The need for the perfect dog was paramount. Owning such a champion would mean a good income for any

The Aire valley – home of the Airedale Terrier.

working man. The men would work with teams of terriers and would bet a 'bob or two'. Of course, the best dog of the bunch could bring in a few shillings, or even guineas, if his owner wanted to sell the animal. The dogs were also used for late-night or early-morning hunting and poaching, bringing back much-needed food for the family cooking-pot.

TERRIER CROSSBREEDING

The Airedale owes its origin to working and middle-class dog owners and breeders who lived in the Aire valley from about 1840 to 1870. There were big terriers in the Leeds/Bradford area around that time which were known to be good companions, strong, adept at catching vermin in the water and fond of hunting.

How was the Airedale produced? It is probably the result of various terriers being crossed with the Otterhound, which provided the Airedale's size and bone. Working terriers, such as the Old English Black and Tan, and the Irish Terrier, contributed expression to the head as well as the rich tan colour. Then there was the Bedlington Terrier (the name originates from Bedlington, a village in Northumberland) which was a speedy and enduring dog, greatly valued by the pitmen (coal miners) for rabbit coursing and dog racing. It is noted in historical records that the Bedlington was crossed with the Otterhound but the results proved disappointing. So, obviously, other terriers must have been involved in the Airedale's development. However, occasional 'Woollies' sometimes present themselves in a litter of Airedales even today. These may have originated from the Bedlington.

The Bull Terrier strain had also been introduced to the Bedlington, for fighting purposes and for rabbit coursing. The Bull Terrier brought in bone, strength, and cat-like feet and was valued for his courage and fighting spirit. Colour and size varied in this breed; some were black and tan with a little white, and some brindled and white. The dogs that fought with Wombwell's Lions (a travelling show that featured hugely

The Airedale has a love of water, and this is thought to come from early cross-breeding with the Otterhound.

popular 'sporting' fights between dogs and imported wild animals) at Warwick in 1825 were said to be large Bull Terriers. Later, dog show enthusiasts preferred the 'milk white' Bull Terrier.

THE EVOLUTION OF THE BREED

The weight of the dog played a great part in hunting. To cross a terrier with a Bull Terrier would give more weight and size to the breed. The resultant dogs weighed 30-35 lbs, compared to the old 15-20 lb hard-coated terrier. These larger and stronger dogs (Bull Terrier and terrier cross) were sometimes pitted and fought against each other.

The Otterhound was introduced once more to help produce a good nose for hunting, plus a fondness for water allied to gameness. Bull and hound crosses, and others back to the Terrier, gave dogs the standard of the day.

The houndy ears were still a main concern, with the complaint that the heads were too narrow and long. It is

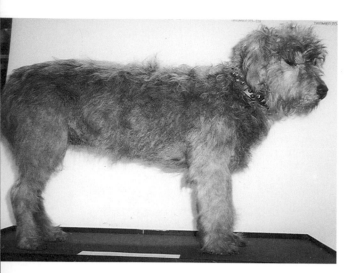

*Bloss: 1887-1900, owned by Thomas Forster.
Photo: Keith Raper, courtesy of the Cliffe
Castle Museum.*

ironic to realise how important this
feature, the head, is by today's standard.
However, at least they were breeding
dogs weighing around 45 lbs. A few
boasted of having dogs weighing 50 lbs,
but these were possibly three-quarters
Bloodhound. The dogs were also
required to be long-legged. This feature
enabled them to work the water edges of
the rivers without having to swim, and
also to climb or jump over the stone walls
of the Yorkshire fields without having to
be lifted.

It will never be ascertained exactly how
the Airedale was fashioned but it was
recorded that it improved faster than
almost any other breed.

In 1872, one Thomas Foster owned a
bitch named Floss. He also owned a dog
named Tick, who had black silky hair
with tan legs and, to complement the
overall picture, he was tan around his
muzzle. These two were mated and
produced a dog pup named Dick. From a
litter sired by Dick came a bitch named
Bess. Foster, who had lived in Bingley,
later moved to Keighley, taking with him
Bess, a bitch of an earlier generation. Bess
was crossed with a black retriever
between the years 1878 and 1881.
Manifold was a product of these matings
and was well known in Bradford, Leeds,
Colne, Nelson and around Skipton and
Airedale. Manifold was reported to be all
black with a 'curly coat'. The idea behind
this breeding was to produce a dog which
would trail and swim, and which was
intelligent, obedient and a trusting
companion.

Foster also owned Bloss, who was of a
similar type to Floss and who lived from
1887 to 1900. She was stuffed and
mounted after her death, and was
eventually presented to Cliffe Castle
Museum, Keighley in Yorkshire, by
Foster's daughter, Miss Foster.

Although her colour has faded with
age, 13 years was an excellent lifespan,
even by today's standards. Bloss
obviously made a great impact on
Thomas Foster, as he had her preserved
for all time, and we are fortunate in being
able to observe one of his early Airedales.
Foster, due to his breeding of a race of
sporting dogs such as Bloss, ranks as one
of the pioneers of the breed and, indeed,
it was he who first named the breed the
Airedale Terrier at Bingley.

WATERSIDE TERRIERS
Around 1870, local dog societies began
classes for what were called 'Waterside
Terriers' at their annual shows. The
Waterside was first named in records
dated 1863. They eventually gained the
highest number of classes and the largest
number of entries on some local
occasions, with nearly as many as 200

entered at one exhibition. Hugh Dalziel, a noted judge and dog fancier, wrote, after judging at the Airedale Agricultural Show held at Bingley in 1879:

"The class for broken-haired Terriers, the Bingley Terrier par excellence, was an exceedingly good one, the dogs being unusually level in character. The winner among the Black and Tan Terriers, Mr B. Swinburne's Slavani, is probably the best dog of its kind that has been produced for many a year."

From a study of some newspaper correspondence, it appears that Hugh Dalziel tried to change the name to the Bingley Terrier, as he had mentioned in his judging at Bingley show. He preferred the name Bingley as it identified the area where he considered the dog had first evolved.

However, many admirers of the breed protested about pinpointing Bingley as the home of the breed. Some called the type the Waterside Terrier; others preferred the Bingley Terrier.

The breed at that time was always well represented at the Bingley show and it was there that, after judging had taken place in 1879, a meeting was called and the name Airedale Terrier was adopted. It was thought more appropriate to call the dog after its area of development rather than a single town.

With the new name acknowledged, fresh interest was created. Other shows made classes for the Airedale, encouraging new competitors to enter the lists and competition was strong. This was obvious from the numbers of people seen around the rings at the Otley and Bingley gatherings.

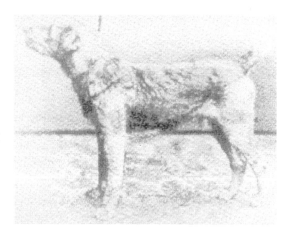

Ch. Cholmondeley Briar (Airedale Jerry – Cholmondeley Luce), bred at Queensbury, near Bradford, UK.

EARLY PARENTAGE
At the time (1879) that Airedales received their present name, one dog called Bruce was at the head of the breed. He was owned by Edward Bairstow, one of the Airedale's original breeders. Bairstow sold Bruce to a Mr C.H. Mason who took him to America.

Mason entered Bruce in a Rough-Haired Terrier Class in New York in 1881 and won a first place. Before he left to become the first Airedale/Waterside/Bingley Terrier in America, Bruce fathered a well-known English dog called Champion Brush, who was blind in one eye, but described as being "an excellent animal in other respects, and a most valuable stud".

In early Airedale lines, a dog called Rattler won many prizes. His dam, Bess, was by Champion Brush, one of the very first dogs exhibited, whose sire, as we have seen, was Edward Bairstow's Bruce. Rattler's son, Airedale Jerry, was very much in the limelight and famous in the breed, but he did not have many of Bess's attributes. The bitches seem to have been less prominent in the early days.

Champion Cholmondeley Briar's dam was Cholmondely Luce. Records give a short but good account of Cholmondeley Luce's qualities. She was said to be "a good-headed one, very terrier-like in character, with small ears and good coat, but a trifle under-sized." It appears that hound ears were a difficult part of the breeding, so this bitch with small ears may have altered many a breeding line!

Many good bloodlines originate from Airedale Jerry (the sire of Champion Cholmondeley Briar). He was said to be "big, strong-boned, a long typical head, hard wiry coat, but overdone in ears".

Cholmondeley Briar started his showing career at the age of six months; he won over a hundred first prizes. He was first exhibited under the name of Red Robin at a local show. F.M.Jowett writes:

"He had a beautiful long clean, typical head with great power in front of the eyes, nice small ears, lovely neck and clean, well-placed shoulders, with good short firm back and well-set, gaily carried tail. His bone and legs and feet were extraordinary, and as round and firm as an English Fox hound's, and being well covered with hair, gave him an appearance of immense strength. In colour he was dense black on his back with rich golden tan on his legs and quarters, and his coat was both straight and hard. He had any amount of substance, yet he was all terrier, with nothing houndy or coarse about him. He was well up to standard weight, and when mature I would say a little over the standard.

"Ch. Cholmondeley Briar will always be remembered by Airedale Terrier breeders, and his name appears in nearly every first-class pedigree of the present day (1913)."

THE PROGRESSIVE YEARS

Around the 1880s it was noted that the Airedale was being carefully bred, and that, as the years progressed, the breeders had shaped and improved him. Few varieties of terrier had made greater progress in popularity than this breed. At this stage in its breeding history it was recorded in *The Illustrated Book of the Dog* by Vero Shaw that:

"Mr Reginald Knight was noted as a practical man with a long-time interest in the breed. He owned a dog named Thunder; this dog was noted as being a true working Airedale terrier. Thunder, after seeing a live rat thrown over the rails of the new Leeds Bridge, on being told to 'fetch it' jumped over into the river after it, a distance of forty to fifty feet. He also stated they make first-rate 'night dogs'. All his dogs would use a low growl if any man were near. Airedale Terriers can kill anything and will do anything. They can be broken to the gun, broken to ferrets; they can go out ratting and will not touch a rat in the net, they will drive sheep and cattle like a sheep dog, fetch and carry like a retriever, hunt like a spaniel, and are as fond of water as a duck and as game as obedient. This is the breed which excels."

Yorkshireman Mr Knight submitted the following Standard to most of the leading admirers and judges of the breed on behalf of himself and his associates.

"Head – Flat and of good width between the ears.

Muzzle – Long, and of good strength; the nose being black, the nostrils large and the lips free from 'flews'.
Mouth – Level teeth large and sound.
Eyes – Small, bright, and dark in colour.
Ears – Thin and somewhat larger, in proportion to the size of the dog, than a Fox-terrier's; carried forward, like the latter's, but set on more towards the side of the head, and devoid of all long, silky hair.
Neck – Strong rather than neat, and free from dewlap and throatiness.
Shoulders – Well sloped.
Chest – Moderately deep, but not too wide.
Hind quarters – Square and showing good development of muscle. Thighs well bent.
Back – Of moderate length, with short and muscular loins.
Ribs – Well sprung and rounded, affording ample scope for the action of the lungs.
Legs – Straight and well furnished with bone.
Feet – Round and with no tendency to 'spread'.
Tail – Stout, and docked from 4 to 7 inches.
Coat – Broken or rough, and close and hard in texture.
Colour – A bluish grey of various shades, from the occiput to root of tail; showing a 'saddle back' of same, also a slight indication on each cheek; rest of the body a good tan, richer on feet, muzzle, and ears than elsewhere.
Weight – From 40 to 45 lbs. for dogs, and from 35 to 50 lbs. for bitches.

"The following gentlemen have signed their names to the following statement:

Illustration of the early Airedale Terrier, from the book 'Modern Dogs' by Rawden B. Lee.

'I agree to the above standard, and will base my decisions on it.'
W. Lort, Fron Goch' Hall, Dec. 1879.
J. Percival, Birmingham, Dec. 3rd 1879.
John Inman, Dec. 3rd 1879.
S.W. Wildman, Bingley, Dec. 9th 1879.
John Fisher, Dec. 3rd 1879.
Edward Sandell, Dec. 1879
J. Speed, Dec. 3rd 1879.
John Crosland, Junr, Wakefield, Dec. 1879.
Charles W. Brinsley, Dec. 10th 1879.
T. Kirby, Dec. 9th 1879.
Reginald Knight, Chappel Allerton, Dec. 1879.

"The standard having received the support and approval of the above and other judges and breeders, it is hoped that others will endeavour to reconcile their views to it, and that the Airedale Terrier will not suffer, as so many other Terriers have done, from a plethora of types, each judge at the same time advocating his own particular prejudices to the injury of the breed.

"The dog selected for illustration is Mr Knight's Thunder, a first-rate specimen of the breed according to the above standard. Thunder is aged four years, and weighs fifty-two pounds, and his measurements are:

"Tip of nose to stop, four and a quarter inches; stop to occiput, five and three-quarter inches; length of back, twenty inches; girth of muzzle, twelve inches; girth of skull, eighteen inches; girth of neck, sixteen inches; girth round brisket, twenty-seven inches; girth round shoulders, twenty-five and a half inches; girth of loin, twenty-two and a half inches; girth of thigh, sixteen and a half inches; girth of forearm, six and three quarter inches; girth round pastern, four and one eighth inches; height at shoulders, twenty and a half inches; height at elbows, twelve inches; height at loins, twenty and three quarter inches; height at hock, six inches."
Illustrated Book of the Dog, 1881

I once read that "If you have this dog after reading this old description, keep it and enjoy the thought that you have bred or owned the perfect specimen!"

There are a few differences in today's Airedale Breed Standard, the scissor bite being introduced later. The height is less than today's Standard, but over the years the Airedale has seen various sizes. I have been approached numerous times by retired Yorkshire miners who have said to me "they were much bigger when I was a lad."

Size was a factor in the early days, when some dogs weighed as much as 60lbs, and others were considered too small, resembling Welsh Terriers.

THE DUAL NAME
The report of the Airedale Agricultural Show held at Bingley in August 1880 was as follows: "The broken-haired Airedale Terrier, a breed much admired in this district from which it takes its name, although not a large class, was exceedingly good, some wiry animals being shown." The judge was Hugh Dalziel, and at this show, he used the name Airedale, coined the previous year, as we have seen. Birmingham provided the breed with a class at the National Dog Show in 1883, where the breed was named the Airedale or Waterside Terrier. This dual cognomen continued for three years, when the latter name was discontinued and the breed became solely the Airedale Terrier, as it remains today. During this period, Airedales were classified in the stud book under Broken Hair Scotch or Yorkshire Terriers.

In 1886, the breed was included in the Kennel Club Stud Book and, unlike some later additions, began well with an entry of 24; with about three exceptions, all had pedigrees – a fact that proved they were worthy of the position in which they were placed.

EARLY SHOWS
At the Crystal Palace Show in 1891, Mr H. M. Bryan's entry of Airedale Terriers were Newbold Test (who was leading winner for some years), Cholmondeley Briar and Cholmondeley Bridesmaid, who shared the special honour of winning the cup for best team of Terriers in the show with Mr Leatham's mustard Dandie Dinmonts, a breed much to the fore at that time. There were 11 batches competing, including Fox Terriers, Irish Terriers, and other popular breeds. This demonstrates the improvement of the Airedale Breed.

STRIVING FOR QUALITY
Holland Buckley was the originator and first secretary of the great UK National Terrier show. He made numerous Airedale Champions under the Clonmel

The Sale of England's Undefeated Champion Airedale

CHAMPION FLORNELL MIXER

A newspaper cutting from 'Our Dogs', January 1926.

prefix with his partner Royston Mills, and many of his dogs were sold abroad, especially to America. He is on record as saying "the very easiest point of all to attain is size, the hardest is quality." He was also critical of coats, many of which were soft or woolly. He preferred coats to be harsh with a thick, oily undercoat, so that the animal can be hours in water without materially altering the feel of the coat.

Many of the old terrier fanciers did not appreciate the cat feet seen on many terriers. They preferred the larger webbed foot of the hound, which was certainly better for swimming. Holland Buckley stated that it was possible to find in the same litter passable examples of the Old English Terrier, the Airedale, the Otterhound and the Welsh Terrier, and dun-coloured specimens still appeared in litters at this time.

Mike Green of Keighley, Yorkshire, a dedicated fancier of the Airedale all his life, brought the following information

to my attention. His father, Joe Green, a much-respected Yorkshireman, was born in Steeton in 1901 and registered Airedales, in most cases with his father, Harry Green. Well-known winners of the time, bred by Mr Green, were: Airedale Nanette, sold to a Mr Corbett of Glasgow; Barrister's Chancellor; his sire, Moorhead Marquis (his sire was Ch. Warland Ditto and his dam was Ranch Girl; her dam was Steeton Peggy). Barrister was bred in 1923 and he was best puppy at Birmingham National. Then there were Briggus Bonnie Boy, Steeton Commander, Airevale Sunster and Briggus Queen, dam of Int. Ch. Briggus Princes who went to the USA and produced many winners.

In 1924, Joe registered Barrister's Duplicate, whose sire was Moorhead Marquis and dam was Steeton Peggy. A short account of Barrister's Duplicate reads: "He was made the best, he has a long clean cut head, good neck, capital body and coat, an undefeated dog." Joe parted with this young winning dog to Mr T. Parkinson of London Road Kennels, Blackburn. He later became known as Ch. Flornell Mixer and was sold to America as "England's undefeated winner", taking the title Int. Ch. Flornell Mixer. He was the sire of 14 English Champions. During his life he sired 27 Champions in England and the USA.

During the 1920s and 30s, movement and communication were difficult. Imagine the inconvenience and expense of public transport to shows, and the hours spent travelling. Stud fees at the time were around three to four guineas. Joe Green became a well-respected breeder and judge. He was noted as being "a pleasant, quiet chap who every now and then springs a new one on us

and is always at or very near the top."
Airedales born in kennels in the Aire
valley survived many long journeys and
some of Joe's breeding joined the
pioneers taking Airedales to the USA.

The Airedale was not without admirers
on the Continent during those years and
was a special favourite in Holland, Russia
and in certain parts of Germany. The
breed took on many different roles, from
hunting big game to guarding duties. It
was an all-rounder.

AIREDALE HEROES

Lt. Col. E.H. Richardson was a great dog
trainer in the early part of the 20th
century. His opinion was that "as a result
of all my work over the years, my
considered judgement is that for all-
round watching and guarding work, the
most reliable dog in size and character is
the Airedale Terrier. This is my opinion,
not only from experience in my private
kennels, but also from that gained during
the time I was Commander of the War
Dog School, during which time hundreds
of dogs of all breeds passed through my
hands for training."

Before World War I, Airedales had
many admirers who knew that the dog
instinctively guarded – so Richardson
trained the breed to guard men in a
serious way. These dogs worked as patrol
dogs with the docks and railway police,
covering nightly patrols of lonely sidings
and wharves.

During 1914-18, Airedales trained by
Lt. Col. Richardson were the among the
first official war dogs to go to France.
The breed was one of the most popular
for sentry, guard and messenger duties.
Important messages carried by the dogs
saved soldiers from many hazards. A
soldier travelling over heavy terrain

*In the First World war, Airedales were
trained as patrol dogs, used for messenger and
sentry duties.*
Photos courtesy: Giulio de Somma.

14

would take as long as an hour to run the distance a dog could cover in under fifteen minutes. Many stories are told of canine gallantry on the field of duty.

One such story tells of Boxer, a large, powerful Airedale, working with Flash, a brindled lurcher at Kemmel Hill in 1918 France. Both dogs were devoted to their keeper, Dixon. He had no hesitation in saying "there is not a better brace of dogs in this or any other country as messenger dogs. Boxer the Airedale is running like an engine. The lurcher bitch Flash beats him on a week's running by twenty minutes which is not a lot, considering the breeds."

Boxer was a staunch, reliable dog, who ran steadily and never let his owner down. His best time was three miles in ten minutes. On one occasion he went over the top with the Kents. Released at 5 am with an important message, he jumped at his keeper Dixon at 5.25 am. A tip-top performance of about four miles; what a great dog! Dogs like Boxer worked in terrible conditions, sometimes running belly-deep in mud and through heavy shellfire to deliver messages for their masters.

RED CROSS
Airedales were used by Red Cross workers to find men in dense woodland and copses. The dogs had to find the soldier, bring back a helmet or anything belonging to the injured man, and then lead help to the spot where he lay.

POLICE DOGS
Lt. Col. Richardson also trained dogs to assist in police patrol duties. In his book, *Forty Years with Dogs*, he states: "Patrol dogs are to assist the policeman in his nightly duties. The class of animal

required is of a very high standard and is not easily come by. It must be obedient and very intelligent and capable of defending the constable if he is attacked. He must on no account be savage."

Richardson realised that animals for this defence work needed to be of good

In Germany Airedales have been trained as safety Search and Rescue dogs. This is Modular Fibu Falouche. Photos courtesy of Robert Bernt.

Ch. Pinto Rum And Coca-cola, bred by Pia Lundberg and Ruth Rudenholt in Sweden. Today, the Airedale has worldwide recognition as the King of Terriers.

size, of good weight for attack or defence, and powerful.

He wrote: "In the Queen's Park Division where they have two splendid Airedales, marked success has attended the introduction of these four-footed officers, with one of them, Bob by name, showing particular aptitude for police work. The constables who have charge of the animals patrol the extensive and quiet Glasgow district of Pollokshields at night, and it is worthy of note that no house burglaries have occurred since the dogs took up duty."

In Liverpool, a local newspaper reported: "The Chief Constable mentioned that one of the Airedales and a Constable were able to effect the arrest of six men who had been attempting to commit a crime."

AMERICA

The Airedale Terrier Club of America (ATCA) was formed in 1900 and Airedales reached a peak in popularity during the 1920s. A factor in this was that Presidents Warren Harding (1921-1923) and Calvin Coolidge (1923-1929) both owned Airedales. The American Canine Corps during World War II used the Airedale as one of their first breeds for training, declaring these dogs intelligent and dedicated to their work.

The Airedale is used for working and hunting in America and Canada, able to hunt bears, raccoons, foxes, rats, wolves etc., and is notably used for Search and Rescue. In an effort to promote and maintain hunting abilities, ATCA formed a working committee in 1987.

SUMMARY

The Airedale is a terrier; he is strong, heroic, the perfect canine machine, with an intelligence found in few other breeds. He is too big to go to earth, but a terrier he shall always remain. His origin, type and character are most definitely due to the legacy of renowned breeders of the past, who learned to value him above any other breed. They variously named him the 'Black & Tan Terrier', 'Waterside Terrier' and 'Bingley Terrier' – but today he is the unmistakable Airedale.

2 CHOOSING AN AIREDALE PUPPY

There are several approaches to the matter of selecting a breeder in your search for a faithful Airedale companion. Never buy on impulse; always try to find a reputable breeder.

Maybe you would enjoy visiting an all-breed Championship show, at which you can talk to the exhibitors, watch the preparation and visit the ringside when judging is taking place. You may encounter a breeder whose kennel has dogs which have that certain appeal you have been looking for. Some Airedales are sturdy all round; some are refined and elegant. It is all a matter of personal taste.

Dog show exhibitors are people who try to maintain breeding to the Airedale Standard, which is the 'blueprint' of the breed. They put every effort into breeding sound and healthy puppies, and each puppy will have had the best start possible. In the litter there could be the next all-time greatest Airedale!

After judging has taken place, have a chat with as many exhibitors as you can, both at ringside and at the benches where the dogs are quietly sleeping!

Most will assist you with all your questions and offer help in your search for an Airedale puppy.

Local breed clubs may provide details of breeders who have puppies for sale. It might mean travelling, in this particular breed, as Airedale folk seem to breed only when they want a puppy.

Monthly magazines and weekly dog newspapers advertise many breeds for sale in the classified sections. These publications also include many interesting topics for the dog fancier: current events, show calendars, canine health information, and breed notes, to mention but a few.

In the UK, the National Airedale Terrier Association compiles and sells an annual Year Book, as do many clubs abroad. These books feature many breeders advertising their kennels. They also contain interesting topics relevant to the breed.

In the US, the national body is the Airedale Terrier Club of America, who will put you in touch with any regional clubs. In other countries, contact your national kennel club for information.

Int. Ch. Big Lady's Intense Dancer: There is little difference in temperament between male and female – both are loyal and affectionate. Photo: Terttu Lardner.

Rus. Ch. Katerina's Land Curry Garry Of Constanta: The male may be territorial if a new dog comes on 'his' property'.

MALE OR FEMALE?

This is a preference which you may have already decided upon. Personally, I do not feel there is very much difference between the personalities of male or female Airedales. Both are affectionate, gentle and intelligent.

If you decide on a female, consider whether her seasons will be a problem. The cycle is usually every six months, though some Airedale bitches come in season about every nine months, and the duration is a period of about three weeks. During this time, a bitch will have to be kept away from any males. This can be a nuisance if you live in an area where neighbourhood dogs may be on the prowl. You can, of course, have your bitch spayed in order to overcome the difficulties of the seasonal cycle. This operation is at the discretion of your vet, who will explain the best time to spay your bitch. There are usually no complications or ill-effects. Your bitch should not alter in appearance or disposition if the operation is carried out on a young animal. The only drawback of early spaying is if your bitch turns out to be a top-quality specimen of the breed. It would be a waste if she were not allowed to produce a litter which would, hopefully, pass on her qualities.

Owning a male has not brought about any problems in our household. He lives with two bitches and he has never marked (passed urine) in our home. If a female is in season, he may not eat as well as usual, but this soon passes. He is back to normal after a couple of days. Another point to mention is that, if an adult male is confronted with a new dog on his patch/home, he will defend his territory to the best of his ability.

VIEWING THE LITTER

The small bundle of joy that is an Airedale puppy is going to be with you for life, so get ready, your life is never going to be the same! One thing is certain, it will never be dull. Your routine will be totally different, and a regular timetable will play a vital role. The knowledge you have gleaned by talking to reputable breeders will, hopefully, have been digested and you will have some insight into the long-term commitments required by this particular breed.

Always make an appointment with the breeder of your choice before visiting, as they have busy schedules. If the breeder has a large demand for puppies, you may have to reserve one in advance. Thus you may have to wait for a puppy or visit other breeders. Remember, the decision is yours.

When you do visit the breeder of your choice to view the litter, the puppies should be of good weight, appear happy, and be kept in a clean environment. This usually determines that those puppies will make healthy and happy pets. They should be well socialised, have a good disposition, and love to be around human adults.

If you feel that the puppies are not what you expect, do not feel obliged to buy in haste. You may have to visit other breeders until you feel satisfied with the care of the puppies and their dam.

Looking at a litter can be awe-inspiring. There are so many virtues that you will be looking for in a puppy, whether the pup is selected as a show prospect (I question this, as no dog can be guaranteed as a show prospect at eight weeks of age), or as a pet and companion, which should be an Airedale puppy's first and foremost role.

Type and temperament should be important considerations in making your choice. In some cases, it is the puppy who chooses his owner. I once had a small litter of three puppies from my bitch, Emerald, and we had made our decision and were keeping two of the three bitch puppies she had delivered. The prospective owner came to the house, where the three pups were all playing in the garden. The puppy for sale came straight up to the visitor and wagged her tail; it was love at first sight for both, and Molly was the puppy she took home with her. Thinking back, Molly was the perfect Airedale for this lady. Both owner and dog are involved in many charity functions and are also doing well in Obedience. Now aged four, Molly has surpassed her owner's goals. She was much slower than other breeds during her early years of training, but now excels in all she is asked to do.

Your chosen breeder will also chat with you on many detailed aspects of the Airedale, such as the day-to-day care of the puppy, vaccination and worming advice, and his personality and feeding requirements.

You will be able to see the litter's dam and this can sometimes give you an insight into your future puppy's size,

It is important to see the mother of the litter. This will give you an indication of temperament as well as adult appearance. Photo: Amanda Bulbeck.

type and personality. Remember, you will have a fully-grown Airedale at around seven to eight months of age, within an inch or two. It is a bonus if you can see both parents of the litter but, in most cases, the stud dog will live in another part of the country. All reputable breeders want to sell their puppies to caring homes; they too will be asking questions about your lifestyle and ability to provide what is required. Bear this in mind, and do not take offence.

The puppies may be running around the room on your first visit, or they may be sleeping after a meal. It is a lovely sight, and many prospective buyers have said to me, "they look like little Rottweilers". This is because Airedale puppies are very nearly all-black except for a little tan around the beard, eyebrows, and the crease in the ear/head, while the bottom half of the legs are tan. This early shade of tan can usually give you a good idea of how deep or pale the colour will be when the puppy is older.

Many breeders will not allow you to handle the puppies. Infections could arise from the fact that you may inadvertently bring into the area the odd germ, for example, if you already have dogs yourself, in the dirt on your shoes. All your clothing has to be clean. If you are a thoughtful person, it is a good idea to be extra-clean when visiting the litter. After all, when a baby is born in hospital you have to wear a gown when visiting or holding it – a puppy is not that much different. Always have the puppies' health uppermost in your mind.

Look at all the puppies and mentally note who is energetic with plenty of get-up-and-go and who is quiet and laid-back. Do not, however, be taken in by first impressions – the pup sitting alone in the corner may seem quiet, but he may be watching his siblings and asking himself, "Which one shall I choose to play with or 'start on' next?" Could this be the worker of the bunch? A couple of pups may be scrapping and you might immediately react by saying, "Are they fighters?" But sometimes two siblings

A puppy that is lively and full of confidence is likely to have a bold, extrovert approach to life.

Photo: Steph Holbrook.

will not back down from each other, both wanting to be top dog. This is no problem in the long run; when separated they could become the two angels of the litter. We had two super bitch puppies who were always fighting. It brings a smile to my face to think of this now, as they both became Champions.

In every litter, there is always a puppy nicknamed 'Bubbles' or 'Personality Plus' and, believe me, there can be more than one. This type of puppy will demand much attention; he will be clever and will most certainly wrap you around his little paws. Puppies form their personalities partly from their owners' caring guidance and the sensitivity that is shown in their formative months of growth.

When we choose our pup or puppies, we look for bubbly personalities and like to see them walk around the room with a certain air about them. The head and neck should be held well, the pup strutting out in a sure and positive manner. The tail should be held on top, even at this age.

An Airedale's future balance and conformation are seen at about six to seven weeks of age. The pup usually shows the backline he will have at maturity, something of the balance and, as mentioned before, a good tail carriage. At seven to eight weeks of age it will therefore be decision time as to which of the available pups you will choose.

PAPERWORK
Before buying a pedigree dog, always ensure it is registered with your national kennel club (AKC in the US, the Kennel Club in the UK). The breeder will sign the registration document when you purchase your puppy. It carries the history of parentage as stated and declared by the breeder. It contains the registered name of the puppy (chosen by the breeder), the dog's personal registration number, the date it was registered, the breed, the sex, date of birth, the date registered, the colour, the sire and dam's name, and the owner of the dog.

Either or both the breeder and the stud dog owner have had the parent animals' hips X-rayed (see Chapter Five: Health Care). The hip scores of the sire and dam will be included on the registration document. Caring breeders want to promote the best of health in their particular breed, and, because of that fact, registration documents may carry one or both of the following endorsements entered by the breeder: (R) – Progeny not for registration; (X) – Not eligible for the issue of an export pedigree.

A breeder who has put the above endorsements on the registration is obliged to tell the buyer and add the information to the sales receipt. The breeder then has to obtain a letter from the purchaser stating that the purchaser is aware of the endorsements and accepts the restrictions.

The breeder will also hand over the puppy's pedigree; this details your dog's ancestry. Each breeder has his or her own format as to the layout of this document. Usually, it is a four- or five-generation pedigree. This is signed and dated by the breeder as true to the best of their knowledge. The new owner can request a certified pedigree produced by computer from the Kennel Club for a small fee.

The affix is a chosen word prefixed to the dog's registered name and is used by breeders to denote their own breeding lines. An affix is granted to a breeder by the Kennel Club. There is an initial charge for the chosen name and then a small annual fee for its upkeep.

PREPARATIONS AND EQUIPMENT
It is best to plan carefully, well in advance of the excitement of bringing your Airedale puppy home. By assessing and, if necessary, adapting your home environment and buying essential equipment before the big day, you will make the arrival of your new family member much easier for all involved.

THE PUPPY'S SLEEPING AREA
The sleeping area is the most important aspect of preparation in the home. This will be your puppy's special place for a long time and he will need to feel safe and secure. Try to site it where the pup will be in contact with you most of the day and ensure that the area is warm, easily cleaned and draughtproof. The best places are the kitchen or the utility room.

You can partition off the allocated area with mesh puppy panels, which clip together to form any size you require. A playpen can be ideal in the very early stages, but Airedale puppies tend to grow out of these very quickly.

BEDS
There are many types of bed to choose from. The size is very important, as it makes sense to buy one which will accommodate a fully-grown Airedale, so consider this when spending at this stage. Plastic beds are easy to clean and can be made softer by means of a blanket folded for comfort. The fur fabric type of bed is not raised from the floor and will need to be washed regularly. A wet dog, even after being dried off with a towel, will retain enough moisture to soak the material, so do not let your dog into this type of bed until he is totally dry.

A plastic bed also needs to have the bedding changed at regular intervals. Wicker baskets and beanbags may look nice, but both can be destroyed by canine teeth and are difficult to clean. These two types of bed, especially the latter, are better bought when the puppy has grown out of the chewing stage, as both can be dangerous, or even lethal, if chewed.

Introduce your puppy to a crate tactfully, and he will soon learn to regard it as his own special den. Photos: Amanda Bulbeck.

BEDDING

There are many types of specialised synthetic bedding available for your puppy or adult dog. Good brands have the advantage of staying dry on top and retaining any moisture underneath. The advantage with this type of machine-washable bedding it that it is quick to dry. After a spin, a quick shake and ten to fifteen minutes on a warm radiator will suffice. Synthetic bedding may be a little more expensive than a woollen blanket but it lasts for years, so proves to be an economical buy.

DOG CRATES

Dog crates or cages are a wise investment and will last for many years. They can be used for car travel or in the home, where they make a secure and comfortable haven throughout the animal's life. They also fold up to a compact size when not in use.

If you are planning to acquire one, it is a good idea to present it to your puppy from the start as his own personal space. The cage door can be left open (except for short periods when you may want the puppy to be securely enclosed). Place your chosen bedding in the back of the cage and newspapers inside at the front. Water and food bowl can be placed in the pen on the newspaper.

The puppy will soon learn he can go in and out at his leisure. The crate must never be used as a punishment area. Your puppy will then use it for the reasons intended – to eat, to sleep and to play in and around. The door can be closed for short periods, with the puppy inside (during house training for example) as puppies tend not to soil their bed area. In the early days, you will find that this approach, with newspapers in front of the sleeping area, will enable your puppy to relieve himself even when the pen door is closed at night when you retire to bed.

The Airedale puppy grows so fast that a crate suitable for a fully-grown dog is necessary. These items of equipment are also ideal when the a puppy or an adult dog is travelling in the car. They fit well into the back of an estate car or hatchback and keep the dog safely confined in familiar surroundings during a journey. After a wet and muddy walk in the countryside, what better place for your Airedale than in his cage – following a towel rub of course! He can curl up on his blanket and sleep throughout the return journey, the bonus for you being a clean car, possibly containing a snoring dog!

Check the garden for safety and security before your puppy arrives home.
Photo: Steph Holbrook.

THE GARDEN

It is vital to thoroughly check your garden before allowing a dog into your home. Fencing and walls must be checked for height and gaps as puppies may try to dig under fencing and adult dogs may become proficient jumpers. (We named one of our dogs Digger because of the former habit, but, fortunately, he did eventually grow out of his digging phase.) Try to check the boundary of your garden before your puppy arrives.

Plants and flowers look lovely in the summer, but remember that puppies learn from touch, and smell – so let forewarned be forearmed! The excited Airedale puppy will probably try to eat everything and anything he can bite into. Decide what is out of bounds and then be consistent. Making your puppy understand what is forbidden in your home and garden is all down to your approach. From the very beginning, speak firmly but with compassion. The word "No" will quickly be sufficient to stop undesirable behaviour. On the other hand, please do remember your Airedale is only a baby and has to be taught.

For safety reasons, it is essential to check the gate most carefully. Are the gaps wide enough for a puppy to squeeze through? Think about attaching a spring to the gate, a simple precaution just in case a visitor forgets to close it! Walk around in the garden and carefully note (then complete) all the jobs that need attention *before* your puppy comes home to his safe new environment!

COLLAR AND LEAD

A collar is most important for your puppy. An Airedale pup will require different sizes as he grows, so remember this when you are buying these items. The first collar that you buy should be light in weight. A long and lightweight lead is also better while your puppy is young.

IDENTIFICATION

On your Airedale's collar you will need to attach a special disk inscribed with your name or the dog's name, plus your telephone number or home address. Many different styles of disks can be bought from your local pet store.

Tattooing is available at your veterinary surgery or via a specialist in the field. They can tattoo either on the inside flap of one of the puppy's ears or on the inside of one of the back legs. I prefer the ear, as it is easier to access! The number allocated to you is placed on a national list which can be consulted should your Airedale go missing.

Microchipping is also available from

your vet. The chip is implanted into the shoulder line of the animal and scanners can check his personal number against a national database. There is no annual fee; after some initial controversy, some authorities now favour this type of labelling. Microchipping is relatively new for pet animals in Britain. Concern about the chip migrating to different parts of the body was – and ten years on still is – a difficulty for many owners, though manufacturers claim newer chips are less likely to migrate.

Many owners and breeders still prefer the tattoo as a perfectly safe identification procedure for dogs. In some parts of Europe, breeders can tattoo their animals with a sequence number allocated to their kennel. This is a sensible approach to labelling their animals. Simple techniques are, in my opinion, the best solution.

FEEDING BOWLS
There is a great choice of size, materials and price when it comes to feeding bowls. You will require one bowl for water and one for food. It is false economy to buy anything other than strong bowls. Plastic bowls are dangerous for puppies, who like to chew them! A pot water-bowl is good while pups are young, as they will find it difficult to tip over.

However, stainless-steel bowls are a very good buy, and last a lifetime. Some are also non-spill and this is a factor worth considering. If you choose a stainless-steel bowl, buy the size that an adult dog would need to hold its food. Your puppy can feed from an old dish out of the kitchen cupboard in the very early stages. A large bowl will be easy for him to eat from at around the four-month stage. Remember that a growing Airedale puppy eats nearly three times as much as a full grown dog.

TOYS
Puppies, like children, need toys for stimulation and to chew; chewing is a natural process. Providing scope for

There are lots of toys to choose from – make sure you buy items that are both safe and durable.

Photo: Amanda Bulbeck.

chewing can be achieved sensibly by choosing appropriate toys, i.e. toys that are easy to pick up in the pup's mouth.

Visit pet stores and choose with care. Always ask which toys are considered the best for puppies. There are many on the market and some are expensive, but safety must be the ultimate criterion for your puppy. Buying cheap toys will prove, in the long term, to be of no value to you or your puppy. You will find yourself replacing broken toys every time you visit town. More importantly, your puppy may chew and swallow a foreign body in a cheap, shoddy toy. This may lead to choking, a visit to the vet, possibly an operation or, in the worst-case scenario, a death sentence for your beloved puppy.

COLLECTING YOUR PUPPY

When the time comes to bring the new puppy home from the breeder, many people ask me: "What is the best method of travelling in the car?" The puppy will feel safe in your arms or lying on your knees with a blanket for comfort. Some new owners prefer to use a medium-sized cardboard box with a blanket in the bottom. This is fine, as long as someone is sitting in the back next to the box. Just remember, do not attempt to collect your puppy without a helper, either to drive or to stay in the back seat with the puppy.

THE FIRST NIGHT

Your Airedale puppy will not be totally happy for the first few days. He may be homesick, missing his littermates and his dam. The only routine he has known has been taken from him.

The allocated space you have carefully prepared will seem terribly frightening to

Your puppy is likely to feel unsettled for the first few days.

him, especially on the first night when everyone has gone to bed. He will not realise he is in the safety of his new and caring owner's home. He may howl and whimper, not knowing what is happening.

Some may say "let him get on with it", but that is a poor start for your new pal. If he cannot adjust quickly, try leaving the radio on low or placing a ticking clock near his sleeping area, possibly well wrapped up in a blanket, to simulate the beating of his mother's heart. If all fails, take him (with his bed) into your bedroom for a few days – just until he has made the transition to his new surroundings. When he has become accustomed to sleeping in the downstairs room throughout the day, he will gradually learn to accept sleeping alone there at night.

Stick to the diet that your puppy is used to, in order to avoid stomach upset.
Photo: Amanda Bulbeck.

YOUR PUPPY'S DIET

The breeder will have given you guidelines to follow in the very early days, covering the puppy's feeding routine, when he is next due for worming, and an idea of what his basic training has involved.

Some breeders put together a hamper of puppy food for you to take home. This will help to settle your puppy into his new family without changing his regular diet and will consist of the particular brand on which the puppy has been reared. He can try different foods when his initial introduction to his new surroundings has been successfully made, but any change of diet must happen gradually over a period of days.

VETERINARY HEALTH CHECK

Make an appointment to visit the vet within 48 hours of purchase, if possible. The puppy will need to be examined to ensure he is of good health and weight for his age. If the pup is not healthy, hopefully the bond between you and him will not have fully formed, which would make it easier to return the puppy to the breeder without question.

The vet will examine your Airedale and explain at what ages he will require his vaccination course (see Chapter Five: Health Care). Booster vaccinations and health checks are important. The protection from an initial course of vaccines does not last for life. Veterinary practices state that, to maintain protection for your dog, a booster must be administered once a year. The booster vaccination is to protect your dog so he is not so susceptible to disease.

Occasional hypersensitivity reactions may occur, as with all vaccines. It should also be remembered that there are certain animals who may not fully respond to vaccination.

WORMING ROUTINE

Your vet will also advise on a worming procedure and the exact amount needed to administer to your puppy. Worming your puppy is important, as even well-reared puppies may have roundworms (see Chapter Five: Health Care). There is much controversy as to how many times the puppy requires worming up to the age of five or six months. I stress the dosage must be exactly correct given the weight of puppy. It can cause considerable harm to a puppy if the incorrect dosage is administered. Adults can be wormed once or twice a year.

The best approach is to follow the advice of your vet, who will be aware of all the local factors affecting the worming of your puppy throughout his life.

3 *CARING FOR YOUR AIREDALE*

A young, vulnerable puppy requires almost the same intensive care as a human baby. The basic essentials are warmth, love, attention, the correct diet, socialisation, a caring and consistent approach to his training through educational play, safe toys and a safe playing area. The type of rearing you give over the crucial months of growth and development will also play an influential part in how the adult dog matures.

FEEDING YOUR PUPPY

It is important to establish a regular routine and stick to it. Whatever feeding pattern and method you adopt, make sure that a water bowl is available at all times. Always keep it in the same place and as fresh as possible.

Growth is rapid during the first six months of life, and it is essential to feed a top-quality, blanced diet. There is a wide range of dog food available, so take advice and choose with care, after initially following the breeder's recommendations. Do not cut corners on cost; always provide a good-quality brand of puppy food at every meal.

Ch. Jokyl Special Delivery: Correct diet and exercise is the key to rearing a healthy adult. Photo: Terttu Lardner.

Pet foods nowadays are prepared by expert animal dieticians. Many trials and much research have resulted in the manufacture of well-balanced diets for dogs at every stage – puppies, adolescents, adults and veterans. I cannot stress enough the value of giving a reputable puppy food at every meal throughout your Airedale's early growing months. Such a puppy formula will be nutritionally balanced to promote growth and healthy condition. Experts have provided this balance in the 'complete' foods available on the market – owners do not need to add extra vitamins.

Meal One
Your Airedale puppy will appreciate a sense of routine in his life, so try to feed at roughly the same times every day. The first meal of the day should be given after the puppy has had a chance to go out. The daily ration of food should be divided equally between all four meals. If your puppy does not eat all his food within 10-15 minutes, clear it away, and start with fresh food at the next meal. Make sure fresh drinking water is available.

Meal Two
The lunchtime meal should be given between 12 noon and 1pm. Remember to check the water bowl.

Meal Three
Provide this at 5-6 pm.

Meal Four
Check the water. Serve your pup his supper an hour before you retire to bed. This will help him settle for the night. Take puppy outside to relieve himself after every meal, but particularly last thing at night.

The routine described above is only a guide, and every puppy is different. Your Airedale will need four meals a day until he is four months of age, and three meals a day until he is around five months of age. Drop a meal by combining lunch and tea, feeding the quantity that your puppy seems to require. From five to six months of age, he will need two meals a day until he is 18 months old. Some owners cut down to one meal a day; others prefer to divide the ration into two meals, and feed morning and evening.

Always feel the puppy's body – his hair can make him appear fat when he may in fact be too thin. He should have a slight covering of fat along his ribs. His back just behind the ribs should be of a good width when feeling from both sides.

PUPPY TREATS
There are many treats you can give your puppy, who will really enjoy this special time with you. For the very young pup use puppy biscuits. You may like to give a carrot, a pear or an apple cut in half. Puppies enjoy such items – but only when they are a little older. It is important that they are supervised when eating the above until you feel confident they can chew them well.

29

A food treat can be used as a training aid.

Photo: Amanda Bulbeck.

When you feel your puppy is old enough, you can introduce a tasty marrow bone or a hard dog biscuit. These are very good to help loosen puppy teeth and make way for the permanent ones. They are also beneficial in helping to keep the teeth and gums clean, by removing tartar and also exercising the jaw. Make sure your Airedale is always supervised when he has a bone.

ROUTINE AND CONSISTENCY
Routine and consistency are the key factors when dealing with your young Airedale and all the family should maintain simple procedures both in everyday life and while training. Airedales should never be pushed to the limit. The result will be a frightened and nervous dog. Use his name as much as possible and decide on simple command words that everyone in the family must use. Let the puppy grow happily, learning through play and the use of his favourite toy or ball. Food is also a good method of training: Airedales always want to please – especially when there is something in it for them.

Be sure not to include too many repetitions when training, as you will bore your puppy. One session of a few minutes, with the aim being achieved well at the end of it, is enough. The puppy will learn a great deal if you are generous with praise at the appropriate time. If he has to be chastised, the word "No", spoken in a firm voice using a growling intonation, is sufficient. He will soon learn to understand the meaning of the word. Always remember: it is useless to reprimand a dog unless you have caught him in the act. To correct a 'wrongdoing' after the

event will only confuse and distress him. The poor dog will never understand why he has been chastised.

All the family can use these simple procedures. Consistency is the key to success.

HOUSE TRAINING
From the moment you bring your Airedale home, the process of constant care and the feeding routine creates a bond between owner and puppy.

Young puppies need to go outdoors many times in the day to perform their bodily functions. Begin toilet training by taking your puppy out about once every hour or so, and always after every mealtime. Always praise him and play with him when he has relieved himself. Decide on the words you want to use when he does this (make sure everyone who deals with the puppy uses the same phrase) and your Airedale will connect the command with the action. This will also build his confidence. You will soon be able to judge how many times will be necessary in a day. Each puppy is different; some become reliably toilet-trained very early and some much later. It is, after all, the same with children, so always be ready with praise and kindness for your puppy. Do remember they have to be mentally as well as physically ready to achieve this training.

Never rub his nose in the 'accident'! Never reprimand him with a rolled-up newspaper or anything else, as this makes a puppy head-shy to the point of becoming withdrawn and hiding in a corner every time you walk in the room. A puppy will cower in the presence of his owner if he is chastised every time he soils in the home. This makes me very sad, as any puppy or adult dog should always greet his owner with a happy outlook.

It is much more helpful to establish a 'safe' place for your puppy indoors – one that can be easily wiped and disinfected if accidents occur. Lay out old newspapers on the floor area you have allocated. Move the papers nearer to the outside door as your puppy progresses with age. If anyone is at fault for accidents, it is the owner who is guilty of not monitoring the small puppy and thinking intelligently. Toilet training can be hard work, but a consistent and loving approach will bring its reward.

LEAD TRAINING

This part of training is a pleasure and to some degree amusing when looking back over the years, but it can be a challenging period for both the experienced and the inexperienced owner.

The best approach is to start as soon as possible, using a very lightweight extra-long lead, about two metres (six feet) in length. By this stage, I presume your puppy will have been accustomed to his collar. Begin in the garden where it is safe and the puppy cannot escape. Attach the lead and follow your puppy wherever he goes, loosely holding on. Do not let him become aware of you holding the lead, or that you are able to restrict his movement. Build up the training period a little each day. Have tidbits available to hold his attention, and use if required. Talk to him and try to keep him at your side. If something attracts his attention and he begins to run, keep at his side or give enough lead so that he can charge off in front. Never let the lead jerk on his neck, as this can damage a young puppy. Also, if he

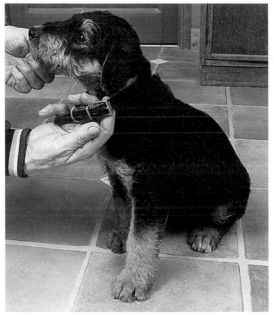

The first step is to accustom your puppy to wearing a collar. Photo: Amanda Bulbeck.

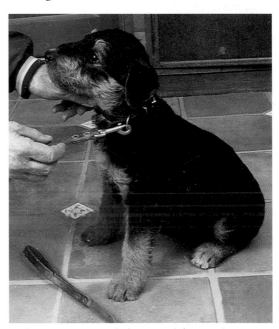

When your puppy is happy with wearing a collar, try attaching a lead. Photo: Amanda Bulbeck.

Lead training can take place in your home or in the garden, and then your puppy will be confident walking on the lead by the time he has completed his inoculations.
Photo: Amanda Bulbeck.

struggles and panics, relax the tension or take the lead off and try another time.

Pursue this approach until he walks happily at your side. If he walks a little in front, there is no problem at this stage – eventually, as his confidence grows, he will want to please you and stay by your side. Make sure he is well adjusted to the lead, socialised to traffic noises and the environment before attempting to take him very far. Sometimes young Airedales will take to the lead like a duck takes to water, but do not be upset if this is not the case with your puppy. Take time out and try every other day or twice in a week. As with other aspects of his development, he has to be mentally ready, so pursue lead training with patience and a kind heart.

Never walk a young puppy for long periods. Ten to fifteen minutes is ample for the socialisation. The garden will provide enough exercise through play until he is around six months old. At twelve months, gradually build up his walks from half an hour to an hour. Always monitor your dog when out for walks, making sure he is fit and well. Never walk too far in hot weather; dogs suffer from excess heat, especially black-coated animals such as Airedales. Try to time your walks for early morning or late evening. On the subject of hot weather, do not leave your Airedale in a room if the sun is full on the windows. Never, ever, leave a dog in the car on hot days even for only a short period; they can die due to heat stress much more quickly than some people believe.

SOCIALISATION
Socialising your puppy is one of the main ingredients in the process of rearing a well-adjusted dog. The inoculation time is one of the main setbacks to this, as your puppy cannot go out until his vaccinations are finished. You can still start on the correct path by allowing him to say hello to visitors. Do not shut him away when friends visit; he is part of the family and should be allowed to mix and socialise. It is wrong for adults and children to lift their hand and swing it down to stroke a puppy. Approaching in this way might make the puppy think you are going to hurt him. Ask people to approach your puppy with their hand held low, the palm facing upwards. They should then let the puppy come to them and should stroke him under his chin; never go for the top of the head. Always teach children to approach dogs in this way. As soon as possible, take your puppy out to meet people, asking them to stroke him but not to pick him up. Puppies wriggle when held and a novice can easily let one fall and injure itself.

If he growls at strangers and tries to snap, stop him immediately, speak harshly to him and say "No", using a growling intonation. Afterwards ask yourself what caused the situation, and try to analyse his reaction. It may be that something was upsetting him, but nevertheless he should never show any aggression. Let him play with other animals, so long as it is without danger for him; he is less likely to become a 'fighter'.

Airedales are curious about their surroundings and need the correct stimulation. Your puppy must also become adjusted to different noises, traffic and the environment. Take him out in the car with you, even if you are only going to the local shops. This will help him become accustomed to the noise and movement of the car. If he is

Exposure to a variety of situations helps a puppy to mature into a well-balanced adult. Photo: Steph Holbrook.

car-sick, try again later and stick to shorter journeys until he has overcome the sickness. He will enjoy a day's outing.

When your puppy is playing he will tire very easily, so do make sure he has a good rest at certain times in the day, e.g. after a meal. This will also help him become accustomed to being alone for short periods. Remember, enjoy your time outdoors together, but do not run his little legs off!

BASIC GROOMING
The care of your puppy's coat is important. It must be kept free of knots in much the same way as when we comb our hair. Invest in a good terrier brush (pin pad) and two sizes of combs, one with wide teeth and one with finer teeth. (For more detailed advice see Chapter Four: Grooming.)

Your puppy must be taught table etiquette, in a gentle manner. This can be achieved by placing him on a grooming table at least twice a week in the early months. Puppies later have to become accustomed to standing for quite a long period when at the grooming parlour, if this is your chosen method of keeping your Airedale well-presented. Any table will suffice as long as it is non-slip and solid. Puppy has to feel safe and happy while this part of his training is accomplished. While he is young and uncertain, it may require two people, one to hold the puppy and the other to brush him. After grooming, treat your puppy as he stands on the table, making it a happy, positive event. Always play with him afterwards, so he understands it is part of his routine. Never lose your temper during grooming – your puppy will never forget and the task will be

33

Grooming should start from an early age. Photo: Amanda Bulbeck.

A comb can be used to work through the coat. Photo: Amanda Bulbeck.

Check your puppy's teeth regularly, particularly when he is teething. Photo: Steph Holbrook.

harder the next time he is placed on a table.

Avoid the stress of matted hair by grooming at least once a week, making sure that each knot is fully combed without pulling. Concentrate on the beard, elbows, chest and hock hairs. The feet need to have the hair between the pads trimmed on a regular basis. The hair can knot badly together, forming lumps that cause the dog to limp with pain, much the same as a stone in your shoe. I cannot stress enough the importance of checking this every month or so.

It is a good habit to get your puppy accustomed to having his feet washed after a walk. Fill a bowl with water and place it outside by the back door in readiness to wash his feet on your return, then dry them with an old towel. This will help avoid problems with the pads – with the added bonus that there will be no dirty paws treading into the house.

Tiny hairs grow inside the ear canal and you must practise dealing with the simple task of their removal yourself; otherwise ask the grooming parlour staff to pull the hairs out carefully. This helps keep the ear canal clear so that air can circulate. Watch for head-shaking, as this can be an early indication of ear problems. Try to remember to pluck out just a few hairs every so often, using your forefinger and thumb.

TEETHING
Teething can be a difficult stage for some Airedale puppies. Always check the teeth to see if any are loose. If your puppy seems to be suffering a little discomfort, use a baby teething gel on his gums. Safe, hard toys are also useful to assist the loose teeth to fall out.

A well-balanced diet is essential for a large energetic breed.

ADULT MAINTENANCE

FEEDING

An Airedale around the age of 18 months will need a diet which will give him all the main ingredients for a long and healthy life. Most foods on the market have been tested for all types of dogs, including special diets for dogs with allergic reactions to certain foods.

Some dogs do not adapt well to a change of diet, so if you decide on a different food, alter it gradually over a period of four to five days. Give three-quarters of his usual food and add to it a quarter of the new food, building up the quantities of the latter and lowering the amounts of the former until you have replaced the original diet completely. The food you give to a house pet need not be as high in protein as that for a working dog or a dog that has long periods of exercise. Only you will know how much protein content your dog requires. Follow the suggested quantities on the can or bag, and notice whether he seems ever-hungry or leaves food at each meal. Otherwise, your hands on his body every week will tell you if the amount you are giving is correct.

WEIGHT

The Airedale is not prone to a weight problem as are some breeds. However, some owners overfeed their dogs. As a breed, Airedale Terriers are active dogs and love to run free and play in the garden or the open fields. Their weight can still be considerable, as some are very heavy-boned and tall. There is no way you can assume your Airedale should be an exact weight. Follow the simple rules – touch and feel his body every time you feed him. There should be a little fat over the ribs but you should be able to feel them without difficulty. Remember, all that hair can deceive even a vet. Airedales can look fat when they are not! From around seven months of age, you will know if he is over- or underweight.

The average weight for a bitch is around 40-50 lbs (18-23 kg) and a dog's weight can vary from 55 lbs (25.5 kg) to as much as 70 lbs (33 kg). Height and bone play an important role. If the dog measures 24-28 ins (61-71 cm) from shoulder to floor, he will be at the top of the weight scale; but if his height is 23-24 ins (58-61 cm), he may only weigh 55-60 lbs (25.5-28 kg). Bitches who are 22 ins (56 cm) from the top of the

Murphee – 28"H 38"L

shoulder to the floor have an average weight between 43 and 48 lbs (19.5-22 kg). Food for thought – a dog lives much longer if he is not obese!

GENERAL CARE

TEETH AND GUMS
Puppies' milk-teeth should be checked, and any loose ones removed. Hard biscuits or a safe knuckle-bone usually help puppy teeth to fall out. The top row of adult teeth should snugly overlap the bottom teeth. This is called a scissor bite. If the teeth are touching equally top and bottom, it is called a level bite: there is no difference to the dog's ability to bite or chew and this is quite a natural jaw.

Sometimes the baby canine teeth may protrude slightly into the upper roof of the mouth. This is not a problem if your puppy has no pain but, if the teeth stop him from chewing, then you should take him to the vet who may snip the point of the tooth until it falls out naturally. The

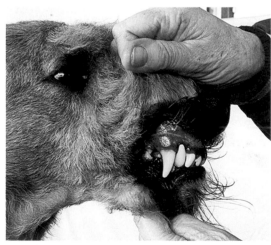

Teeth will need regular brushing to avoid the build up of tartar.
Photo: Amanda Bulbeck.

puppy's jaw is growing and in no way will it mean he will suffer later in life.

Adult dogs need to have their teeth brushed every so often to help stop tartar, decay and bad breath. Buy a canine toothpaste and use it regularly so your Airedale becomes accustomed to it. If tartar builds up severely, the teeth need to be scraped clean. You can do this yourself if your dog is accustomed to having his mouth checked (I hope he is). If not, veterinary help is advisable. A bone to chew will keep teeth clean. Gums should be checked regularly for healthy colour and to ensure that no foreign bodies have lodged between teeth or in the gum, e.g. pieces of chewed sticks or bone.

EYES
The eye tells all. If an Airedale is unwell, the eyes will be dull. If the eyes are sore, look closely to see that no eyelashes are on the rim of the eyelid. Sometimes Airedales suffer with a few eyelashes growing on the rim which can cause discomfort. If you see small but visible eyelashes on the lid, visit the vet (see Chapter Five: Health Care). Sometimes discharge can be caused by small particles of dust.

EARS
Ears need to be kept clean. This can be done using cotton-wool, but make sure you do not probe into the ear canal.

NAILS
Toenails need to be kept short and neat. It is really upsetting to see dogs with long nails, as it is very uncomfortable for them. More roadwork helps to keep them short, but if they do grow too long, they will need to be clipped. This

EXERCISING YOUR AIREDALE
There is no greater pleasure than watching a happy, healthy Airedale running, playing – and swimming...

can be done using guillotine nail-clippers, ensuring that you only trim the tip of the nail. If you cut into the quick of the nail, it will bleed. For first-time owners, it is advisable to ask the vet or your groomer to trim the nails for you.

TOUCH

If your dog is unwell and you do not know the reason, touch him gently all over his body: legs, feet, head, ears, mouth, etc. He will soon let you know where it hurts, either by a little whimper or a growl if you touch a certain part of his anatomy. This may indicate that he requires veterinary help.

HEALTH CHECKS

The best time to give your dog an all-over health check is when you are grooming, when you can feel for any lumps under the hair. Always keep a regular check on your dog's health and condition – problems spotted early are much easier to treat.

EXERCISE

The happiness of an Airedale in full run is something you never forget; likewise when he wants to play and swings around in circles with his rear end nearly touching the floor. I call this bunny hopping. Exercise is good for you and your dog and prevents boredom.

THE OLDER DOG

Take your aged companion to visit the vet about once a year. Old age is not a disease; it is a process caused by a progressive reduction in the efficiency and number of cells in the body. Some diseases become more common as a dog ages and, if detected early enough, they can be treated before they become a real problem. Drinking a lot of water which leads to incontinence during the night is just one of the problems in old age.

From about twelve years of age I like to feed my oldies three times a day, as they enjoy food and it is a way for me to say "I realise that a walk other than gentle exercise in the garden is too much now, especially on hot days." On a good day they love a short car ride and a very slow amble at their own pace around the woods and fields.

Do not let your old dog jump from the car; always lift an old dog out carefully. His bed should be raised a little from the floor and well padded for extra comfort, in a warm, draught-free area.

Try to keep the older Airedale groomed just enough for comfort. It need not be a precision trim – just enough to keep him free from tangles and knots. Toenails will grow long without much exercise, so keep them short and remember to clip the hair from inside the pads.

Finally, not an easy subject, but one which must be addressed. If continuing illness or poor quality of life is facing your dear companion, your vet may suggest euthanasia. The time has come for you, as a caring owner, to make the correct decision. This will be the most distressing decision you will have to make, but you owe it to your Airedale to let him depart without pain or suffering. This can be done in your own home in surroundings which are familiar to him, if you wish, and I would sincerely recommend it from personal experience.

4 *GROOMING*

As we have seen, grooming is a large part of caring for an Airedale and it is worth trying to do things correctly from the start. This chapter will cover in detail how to present the breed in show trim. Even if you never plan to show your Airedale, it is worth knowing how to make these dogs look their best. Do not worry if it seems daunting at first – like most skills, you will improve with experience and by listening to advice.

EQUIPMENT
Pin pad/terrier brush – you will use this brush throughout your grooming but it will not totally release bad tangles and knots.

Stripping blades – buy two stripping blades (until you find which blade sits best in your hand and is easiest to work with): one for close work and one wide-toothed blade (e.g. number 29 or 30) for the jacket and legs.

Combs – you will need one with extra-wide teeth for the legs and beard hair. An undercoat rake will help remove undercoat from the body and dead hair from the legs.

Hound glove – this comes in several forms but the horsehair type of glove is good for the final polish after grooming as it removes debris left in the coat.

White chalk – this is used to help grip the hair when hand-stripping the neck, head and shoulders.

Scissors – for the final finish, under the chin, anus and some areas of the tail, the edge of the ear and around/inside the pads.

De-matting comb (only if required) – it will cut through knots/matted hair and break them down, making the hair easier to brush. Care must be taken when using this tool. Keep the blunt part of the tool against the dog's body, never turn it the other way or it will cut your Airedale.

HAND-STRIPPING
The novice may find it hard to understand or to grasp the overall picture when it comes to hand-stripping (the

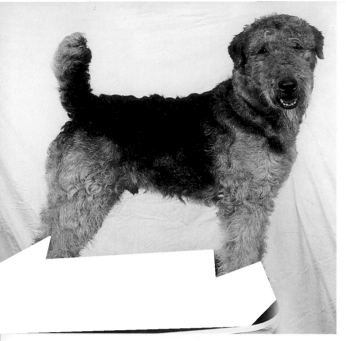

An adult male ready for stripping.
Photo: Amanda Bulbeck.

regular removal of loose, excess hair from the coat). Hand-stripping is a skilled task that requires many hours to achieve the finish that you see in the show ring. I do not believe that there is an Airedale exhibitor who is totally satisfied with the presentation of their dog every time he is exhibited. Please do not judge us too harshly if a dog is not in pristine condition in the ring – even Airedale enthusiasts are only human!

I think back and remember the people who were so much help to me in the beginning. This is why I suggest you talk to the breeder of your puppy if they exhibit. Ask if you may watch them prepare a dog for the show ring.

It may be that you will decide to use a grooming parlour in your area if you are not bitten by the dog-show bug. Grooming parlours can make your Airedale look presentable and clean. Or you may decide to use shears and groom the dog yourself.

Let us look closely at the presentation of our King of Terriers. For the brave, a large picture or photograph on your wall of a Airedale in show trim will help.

LEARNING THE TECHNIQUES
Begin grooming your puppy at 10-12 weeks of age, by which time he will have settled in well and you will have gained his confidence. Your first goal in these early stages is simply to keep the coat flat. This is achieved by brushing the coat well with the pin brush, then using a fine comb through all of the jacket. A fine comb is good at this stage as it helps to rid the jacket of a little of the undercoat. Open your fingers and place your hand on the jacket, starting at the base of the tail. Now push all the jacket hair the wrong way. You will notice longer hair along the topline and down the sides of the coat. Finger-pull (forefinger and thumb) the long hairs out, pulling only in the direction in which the hair lies.

Brush the legs and face. Use a fine comb after brushing, which helps to remove any knots or dead hair in the legs, elbows and face. Take extra care around the foot and behind the pad as this can knot easily. Begin by taking only any long straggly hair from the legs. Do not work on the puppy for long periods on the grooming table. When you have finished, it is time for play and a food treat; make grooming a happy event.

When your puppy is around five to six months of age and is able to stand on the table without a second person helping to hold him safe, it is time to begin the process of helping to make him look like the King of Terriers.

Some breeders advocate stripping the coat down to nearly bare skin, but I feel this is far too severe for a young puppy. The other objection is that the hair will all grow at the same rate and you will not be able to strip by the 'brickwork' method (this means each time there will be old hair to take off while some new hair has already grown). Also, if you have been working on the coat from the age of ten weeks, it should be of a good harsh texture by the age of six to eight months, sometimes earlier.

To achieve successfully the basic hand stripping of your Airedale, begin by brushing the dog all over with your pin brush, then comb all the way through, brushing and combing any knots very carefully, especially at the elbows and the pastern.

A good tip is to pretend you are preparing for a show at the weekend, so you will not have a dog waiting for a coat to grow. This is what can happen if the time factor has not been carefully taken into account. There are many kennels who have been in this situation. Mine is one of them! Let me assure you showing is an expensive hobby. Entry fees are not cheap. If your dog is not ready for the show, do not take him! For hand-stripped breeds the early closing date for entry is the main cause of absenteeism at any major Championship show. One never wants to take a dog in the ring untidy!

THE JACKET
Try to work on the coat every week, using a wide-toothed stripping blade (number 29/30 is my suggestion).

Begin stripping from behind the head at the occiput and pull any long and dead hairs out of the coat by use of finger and

Adult male after stripping.
Photo: Amanda Bulbeck.

41

Areas for stripping, showing where the length of the coat should be stripped to – short, moderate or long. It is essential that the different coat lengths blend in as naturally as possible.

■ *Short* ■ *Moderate* □ *Longer*

The coat is blended from shoulder to elbow, creating the straight lines of the terrier front.

thumb (as mentioned above) or with the wide-toothed stripping blade. Try to take a little of the undercoat using the blade as you proceed. Work along the coat to the base of the tail, keeping in your mind's eye the contours of the shoulder and a level topline. Think of a triangle from the occiput widening towards the top of the shoulder blades. This will show an elegant neck.

Proceed to work on the sides of the jacket. The sides are sometimes not as harsh in a puppy as the topline, so do take care when stripping these areas. Remember to blend coat hair into the shoulders when meeting the rib cage.

Now you have accomplished stripping all the coat, are you tired? Take a break and do not forget to take your dog into the garden for a play time, both relaxing together. Break over, it is back to the grooming table.

This clarifies the areas where to trim short and where to blend. Scissor around the anus (and the testicles in males). The area inside the back legs towards the feet may be scissored or lightly hand-stripped, which will keep the fullness of the leg hair.

Talk to your Airedale all the time, sing to him, give him a cuddle! Brush the coat once more (I hope he is standing well for you – he will get better with time). Begin with your stripping blade and carefully rake out a little more of the undercoat. Do not apply too much pressure as you will hurt and graze the dog's skin. Until he is older, you may prefer to use only a fine comb when raking out the undercoat.

The undertuck can be pulled a little for shaping and scissoring to the required length by starting at the elbow level (the approximate depth) and working up to the abdomen in a gradual line. Try to look at good photographs when scissoring the undertuck as this is an important part of presentation. The dog can look fat if the coat is not correctly tucked up (yes, I have been there and done it). Try to take a little from the length, and either ask someone to hold the dog for you in a stacked position (i.e. the show stance), or let him exercise free to make sure the lay of the hair is correct. Be sure it blends into the jacket, and ask yourself does it appear too heavy or too refined! Your eye for presentation will become better with time.

At the end of the session, your hands and fingers will probably feel sore. Tomorrow is another day. No sitting down yet – reward your Airedale for his patience with garden play or a short walk, and let him stretch out.

HEAD, NECK and SHOULDERS

Another grooming day has dawned, and timing is the prime concern for these three areas. Tackle them around eight to ten days before the show, depending on the growth of your dog's hair.

Try to strip very close to show off a clean head, neck and shoulder/front and always pull the hair in the direction it grows. The use of white chalk dusted over these areas makes the job easier. Again, look at a good photograph and try to follow the lines.

Begin behind the occiput from the imaginary triangular lines we used for the jacket (occiput to shoulder). From here, continue and begin stripping close on both sides of the neck working towards and stripping the front of the neck and also the shoulders.

Follow the lines on the shoulders to where you must blend in with the top of the shoulder. You also need to blend into the ribs and learn where to stop when blending into the top of the leg hair.

Comb away the hair from eye to mouth and begin behind this imaginary line to proceed close stripping of the cheeks towards the ears. Continue around the head again, making an imaginary line above the eyebrows. Comb forward and leave until all the head is stripped close. All these aspects can make or break the presentation of the Airedale.

THE FRONT LEGS

The front legs have to be finger-pulled to gain the fullness required to finish the appearance. Comb the leg hair out to the sides until you have worked all the way around the leg. Pull out hair that is too long or straggly. Imagine a larger-than-life rolling pin; the legs should be trimmed to that type of roundness

Blend the leg hair when viewed from the front (shoulder/elbow/leg); it should show a straight line when correctly trimmed. Hair around the elbow needs thinning carefully as this grows profusely.

On the inside of the front legs, as viewed from the front, comb both the legs so the hair is nearly touching. Pull long straggly hair from the top of the leg working in a straight line towards the feet.

THE FEET

Clean between the pads by cutting any knotted hair, and scissor the hair around the feet, showing a little of the two front nails. This makes the feet look attractive as they should be – round, tight, and cat-like.

THE HINDQUARTERS

The hindquarters are a little more difficult. Start at the base of the tail and pull out the hair, following the lines of your dog towards the bend of the stifle and the hock. Try to keep an even layer of hair on the leg throughout this process. Move to the side of your dog and blend from the coupling towards the buttock.

Just below this area, blend towards the outside angles so as to produce the required shaping all down the outside of the leg. The legs when viewed from the rear should look like a horseshoe. Trim carefully the long hair as you comb it forward to shape it at the front of the stifle towards the feet. Trim feet as before, to make them tight in appearance, but do not show any nail.

When viewing from the back, trim inside the legs again by combing the leg hair in towards each leg and pulling out any long hairs to form a straight line towards the foot. Scissor to the required shape. At the top, inside the back legs, trim closely around the vulva or testicles very carefully with blunt-ended scissors.

The hock hair adds the shape to the angles when viewed from the side. Try to allow this hair to grow a good length.

Finger-pull only the long hair to form the desired effect.

THE TAIL

This is trimmed by pulling the black hair on top evenly, taking out the dead hair to the tip. Work on this area the same as you would on the jacket.

The underside of the tail can be scissored (if you are not showing) evenly to the tip. Trim the length of the hair at the tip by cutting in a semicircle making it neat in appearance. Scissor around the anus carefully.

EXPRESSION OF THE HEAD

I have left this for last, as it is a work of art to achieve the true terrier expression. Begin by brushing and then combing through the hair well enough to release any tangles. Work from the corner of the eye towards the mouth by blending into the cheeks. The foreface must be shaped with finger and thumb, taking care as you work. This hair takes a long time to grow, so do only a little at a time. Look at the expression, then take a little more off until you attain the desired effect. Leave the shaping of the eyebrows until last. Comb them out of the way until you are ready for the final finish. Pull the hair between the eyes carefully. Think of a fairly wide-based triangle as you proceed from between the eyes towards the top of the brow, pulling only a few hairs at a time.

From the side, view the head, and comb the hair up in line from between the eyes to the nose. Finger-pull, trying to keep a straight line from the eye, and keeping the hair of equal length as you work towards the nose. Comb the eyebrows forward and thin out carefully with finger and thumb only, pulling just

■ *Short* ■ *Moderate* □ *Longer*

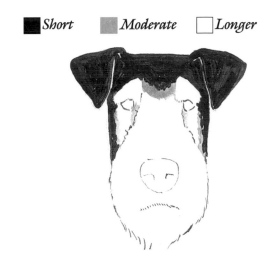

Trim the dark areas very short. From the eye to the mouth, blend the hair into the cheeks. Around the eyes, finger-pull carefully. Finger-pull the eyebrows to the required shape.

Between the eyebrows, blend to the line of the skull. From the outer corner of the eye, finger-pull any fullness to blend towards the foreface.

a few hairs at the corner of the outside eye. Under the chin, make an imaginary line at which to stop stripping. Then blend with scissors to make the flowing lines of the beard when viewed from the side.

Remember, if at first you do not succeed with the expression, your Airedale's hair will grow again and you can have another bash! With practice you will become more proficient.

EARS
These are stripped closely on top, scissored or hand-stripped inside, and carefully scissored (holding the edge of the ear with opposite finger and thumb) around the edges to give a crisp, neat finish. Clear the inside of the ear canal by pulling a few hairs which grow deep inside using your forefinger and thumb. This will help to keep the ear canal healthy. Try not to let any loose hair fall into the ear canal. You can purchase ear plugs for this purpose.

SHEARING
If hand-stripping is not for you, shearing of Airedale coat is an easy process and less tiring for both owner and dog. I have seen dogs sheared and they can look very good, still keeping the black jacket (my own veteran of Jokyl/Shadli breeding is sheared and has a lovely black jacket). However, some jackets after shearing can turn a very light grey in colour.

If all you want is for your dog to be comfortable and clean, then this is the type of grooming for you. It is also better for the older dog as less time is spent on the table.

If you decide to groom the dog yourself, it is wise to invest in a good-quality set of electric shears. There are many on the market to suit any pocket. Over a period of years they will pay for themselves by recouping the cost of visits to the grooming parlour. The attaching blades are sold in different sizes for different parts of the body and will require sharpening every so often, depending on how many times a year

MINIMISING FAULTS

Conformation faults can be minimised with judicious stripping.

◼ *Short* ▦ *Moderate* ☐ *Longer*

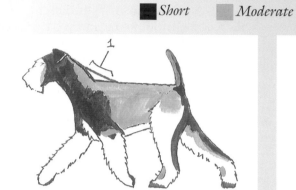

Straight shoulder.

Roach back.

Straight stifle/narrow chest.

Drooping croup.

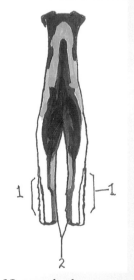

Narrow hocks.

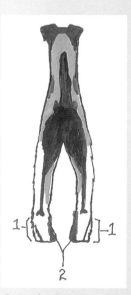

Open hocks.

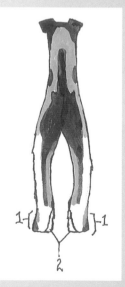

Cow hocks.

Wide front.

they are used. You can begin buying just two blades, one for the body hair and one that will cut closer but not too close for the rest of the body parts. If you use a close blade, it may cause the dog to suffer a type of barber's rash. He may scratch at the area that has been sheared too closely and this can cause a skin irritation. There are antiseptic sprays and creams to use after shearing to help soothe canine skin.

When you have finished shearing your dog's jacket, head, neck, shoulders, rear and ears, rake the jacket with a fine comb or wide-toothed stripping blade to clear the undercoat. This helps to maintain the jacket's true colour. The legs are better hand/blade-stripped as explained above in the hand-stripping section. The Airedale's lovely contours are shown to advantage by good leg furnishings. Also you have the satisfaction of grooming him yourself and can conduct a medical check-up at the same time. Do not forget to clear the hairs from inside the ear canal and between his foot pads every time you groom.

THE GROOMING PARLOUR
Canine grooming parlours have qualified staff who can trim and bath any dog. They have a gentle but firm approach to animals. Grooming parlours work on an appointment system, so do make sure you book well in advance.

Before doing so, make sure you have trained your Airedale to stand on a table to be brushed. If you have not, you may have a very sad animal to greet you on your return.

The staff will have had to work very hard to keep him still. When you take your Airedale for the first time, do not take him uncombed. It is the owner's job to keep him free from tangles. When you collect him from the parlour, be aware of how he greets you. Is he happy? If you feel they made have a good job of your pet, you could make a regular appointment for every eight to ten weeks. Remind the grooming parlour to clean the ears well inside and to clip the nails when necessary. Prices vary from area to area, but it is worth the money if you have a busy lifestyle.

5 *HEALTH CARE*

BASIC FIRST AID
This constitutes emergency measures to save life, ease pain and suffering and aid recovery while professional help is awaited. First aid is generally valuable in sudden illness and after accidents. In order to save critical time, it is advisable to keep a first-aid box stocked for the dog. Many items you store in your own first-aid box may be of use for your Airedale.

ASSESSING ILLNESS
Airedales are healthy animals but some do have health problems. Every owner wants a healthy pet, but dogs may suffer illness from time to time. You will notice when he is unwell; he may be lethargic and introverted and his appetite may decrease or increase.

SIGNS OF ILLNESS
Main signs are: panting without reason; ears twitching back; looking off-colour; drinking abnormal amounts of water; vomiting; diarrhoea; breathing difficulties or coughing; bleeding (any area); scratching; eyes discharging/sore/swollen/sensitive to light; head-shaking; ear discharge or swollen ear flap; limping; blood-streaked or too frequent urination; loose bowels or pain on evacuating.

ACUTE SIGNS
Consult the vet immediately if any of the following occur: collapse; severe vomiting or diarrhoea (or both) for more than 24 hours (there may be a need to go earlier than this!); cramp; trouble breathing; bleeding; signs of severe pain or discomfort; drinking abnormal amounts; heatstroke.

If you have any urgent cause for concern, especially in puppies or older dogs, seek treatment immediately.

At the surgery, it will help your vet if you can give an accurate history of your dog's condition. Some people write it all down – just in case. The vet will give a physical examination, looking for lumps and bumps, the colour of the membranes (the lining of the lips and eyes), teeth, gums, ears, skin temperature, and more.

Sometimes aids will be needed, e.g. X-ray or a blood test, either to confirm what the vet thinks or to help in reaching a positive diagnosis of the dog's illness.

Carole Kane (Hollytroy Airedales, Canada) with ten-month-old Zorro.
Every owner has responsibility for their dog's health and well-being.

PARASITES

ENDOPARASITES (internal)
WORMS

Regular worming should take place about every six months for an adult dog who is in close contact with children, but once a year is sufficient otherwise. Worms can cause a dull coat, swelling of the stomach, loss of weight, pneumonia and diarrhoea. In addition, one of the commonest roundworms, Toxocara canis, is easily transmitted to children, and can cause potentially permanent eye damage. A multi-wormer bought from your veterinary surgery will rid the dog of all types of worms. It is worth mentioning that you must weigh the animal accurately in order to administer this type of drug correctly, as overdose is possible. Be totally sure; read the label and only give the exact amount.

Puppies up to six months need a gentle wormer, a ten per cent liquid given over three days or similar. Some wormers sold commercially are much too strong for young, sensitive stomachs. Never worm during a vaccination course – it will put too much strain on the system of a puppy or an adult dog, so wait a few weeks.

However effective the wormer recommended by your vet, re-infestation can occur from the environment. Please do remember these simple precautions to reduce the spread of parasites.
1. Effective flea control for the animal and your home – this helps reduce the transmission of the flea tapeworm.
2. Clean up faeces straightaway – always carry a strong plastic bag or poop-scoop.
3. Avoid raw offal.
4. Train your dog to use a certain toilet area in your garden and keep children away from the area.

HEARTWORMS

These parasites are transmitted during the larval stage by mosquitoes and are endemic to tropical and subtropical areas. Only rarely do they occur in the UK and Europe. In the US, they were once thought to exist only in southern states but they are steadily expanding their range. The larvae enter the dog's bloodstream and develop into worms. They, in turn, lodge in the heart where they interfere with the pumping of blood. The presence of microfilia (larvae) can be detected by examination of a blood sample. Symptoms include coughing and general lethargy. Prevention can be achieved by treatment once a month.

ECTOPARASITES (external)
FLEAS
Fleas on a dog are different from those which infest humans and cats. A flea bites and injects saliva to stop the blood clotting while it is sucked up. The saliva contains chemicals, which can cause an allergic reaction in the dog.

What to look for: black gritty material in the coat; bites which look like small red pimples; in sensitive dogs, large areas of inflammation on the dog's back. Spray and bath treatments can be bought from your veterinary surgery – again, read the instructions carefully. When using a spray, try to use it outside with the wind blowing away from both you and your pet, and try not to inhale any! A household spray can also be used to treat the pet's bed area and your home frequently throughout the summer months.

There are other tried and tested remedies. Six drops of lavender and two drops of tea tree oil, mixed with two tablespoonfuls of water and shaken well in a spray container, makes an effective anti-flea mixture. Spray the dog's coat, bedding and carpets. This has the advantage of smelling good! Also try garlic tablets and brewer's yeast (or garlic and fenugreek tablets) or an Oil of Olay soap bar to bath your Airedale.

LICE
There are two types of louse: biting lice, which chew on skin flakes, and sucking lice. The latter cause skin irritation as they penetrate the dog's skin and feed on tissue fluids (neither will spread to humans or cats). Lice are grey and lay small eggs which stick to the dog's hair.

Treatment is by giving sprays or baths three or four times at five- to seven-day intervals. This will kill adult lice and any hatching larvae.

TICKS
The sheep tick is the most common tick seen on dogs. It has a large abdomen that fills with blood as it sucks with its mouthpart through the skin. It hangs on the dog's hair, usually on the underside, between the forelegs and on the head. In the US, dogs have to contend with several forms of dog-specific ticks. The common brown tick is found in most areas, as well as deer ticks.

It is important to remove the head of the tick or an abscess may form. If the head is left in, warm compresses may help to draw out the infection, combined with antibacterial washes and creams. It is not an easy task to remove ticks. Flea spray used locally means the tick will die and can be removed the next day. Another method is to dab the tick with alcohol (gin or methylated spirits). Wait a few minutes and dislodge it. Ticks have a screw-like structure on their heads and bore into skin tissues by turning anti-clockwise, releasing themselves by turning clockwise. A tick can therefore be 'unscrewed' by turning it round several times in a clockwise direction, applying gentle traction. The head with its dreaded pincers does not tear off with this method, thus avoiding complications such as dermatitis or an abscess.

EAR MITES
These mites live in the canal leading to the eardrum and cause intense irritation. They can be treated with proprietary medications. If your dog is shaking his head constantly and is suffering discomfort, a check by the vet will be required.

Ch. Saredon Jennifer Eccles: Joint top-winning Airedale in the UK, 1997.

MANGE

There are two types of mange found in dogs – demodectic and sarcoptic. The latter is the worse. The mites which cause sarcoptic mange burrow deeply into the skin and lay their eggs. Once infestation develops, scabs form (scabies). Loss of hair and thickened or wrinkly skin ensues and itching becomes very severe. If left untreated, complications can set in. It is wise to follow the vet's instructions to the letter when treating both the dog and your home.

INFECTIOUS DISEASES

VACCINATION

Animals, like humans, can benefit from a vaccination regime, to counter infectious diseases. I always feel the need to do the best for our animals, starting with young puppies and continuing throughout their adult lives. Bear in mind that protection given by an initial course of vaccines does not last for life, and to maintain protection it is essential that your dog has a booster vaccination once every year. (At the time of writing, there is much controversy as to how soon after canine initial vaccination an annual booster is required.)

A small number of animals may fail to respond to vaccination and some develop allergies. Vaccination routines vary from one country to another but, in the main, all dogs receive the same vaccines worldwide. They are administered for protection for the following infections, which may arise in your own locality.

DISTEMPER

Canine distemper is a serious viral disease, which attacks the nervous system of dogs, foxes and members of the Mustelidae family, including badgers, ferrets, stoats and mink. It is highly infectious, especially among young dogs, although it can be contracted by dogs of all ages. Those between three and 12 months are the most vulnerable.

Symptoms include a rise in temperature and a thickening discharge from nostrils and eyes. The dog becomes lethargic, depressed and loses interest in food. Respiratory complications may arise (including cough, bronchitis and severe bronchopneumonia) or those of intestinal origin (including diarrhoea, vomiting and abdominal infection), depending on secondary attack by bacteria. In some forms of the disease, the pads of the feet become swollen, thick and hard, a condition known as 'hard pad'. Nervous conditions may also be present, especially in the later stages and sometimes convulsions occur, with paralysis following. Distemper is better prevented than treated, since treatment is rarely effective and the disease often proves fatal. Even if the dog is lucky enough to recover through the use of medication, followed by extreme care in convalescence to prevent rapid relapse, complications may arise in later life. Immunisation at ten to 12 weeks of age provides protection and regular boosters are advisable. No puppy should be allowed in public prior to immunisation for fear of contracting distemper (or other serious diseases such as hepatitis and leptospirosis).

Widespread immunisation in the past has substantially contributed to the rarity of distemper in modern times.

INFECTIOUS CANINE HEPATITIS

This condition involves inflammation of the liver. Infectious canine hepatitis, caused by a virus, can be lethal and frequently occurs with distemper. A combined vaccine is available for protection and this can be given when puppies receive their vaccination, routinely at eight to 12 weeks of age.

Symptoms vary but include gastrointestinal haemorrhage, vomiting, diarrhoea, listlessness, high temperature, thready pulse and abdominal tenderness.

LEPTOSPIROSIS

A dangerous disease with a high mortality rate. Immunisation in puppyhood is the best preventative method. Leptospirosis is caused primarily by contact with infected rat urine, but transmission is also possible from one infected dog to another and the disease can be prevalent among kennelled puppies. One form of the disease is called 'infectious jaundice'. Symptoms include the characteristic yellow tinge to mucous membranes common in jaundice, as well as vomiting and clay-coloured or dark, stained faeces, which smell foul. The dog may also develop diarrhoea or gastrointestinal bleeding and the kidneys may become damaged. Dogs which recover may carry residual infection in their kidneys for up to three years.

Having experienced this disease at first hand, I have to admit you have no time to think about your next move. One of my puppies at 12 weeks old did not eat with the others, so I took her out of the kennel to feed her. She ate for a couple of minutes, then vomited. Without hesitation I took her immediately off to my vet, who took blood samples but mentioned he suspected lepto. She was diagnosed and put on a drip. Within 12 hours, she had died. We had taken every precautionary measure, but it only takes one rat – or even a snail – to cause a death. A procedure used by many kennels is to upturn water bowls at night so rats cannot urinate in them. Remove any food.

The lesson is: if your puppy shows any of the symptoms, head straight for your vet.

PARVO AND CORONA VIRUSES

These are deadly viral infections for dogs. Young puppies and older dogs are more at risk. Parks where many dogs are walked are high-risk areas and any faeces on your shoes can carry the infection into your home.

Symptoms are lethargy, vomiting, blood in faeces or diarrhoea. Seek veterinary help immediately.

INFECTIOUS BRONCHITIS

A name now used for bronchial infections in dogs, far more appropriate than 'kennel cough'. That term, used in the past, implied it only came from boarding kennels, but dogs are just as likely to become infected at dog shows, training classes, parks, or even at the veterinary surgery – after all, that is where you would go if your dog is constantly coughing. So please, do not only blame kennels; a particular dog has to bring the infection in! If you suspect a cough, tell your vet before you enter the waiting-room with your dog: this condition is highly infectious and you must consider the other patients or any animal you come into contact with.

The cough can be harsh and dry, and begin quite suddenly, sounding as if a foreign body is stuck in the throat or the dog is about to vomit. Breathing heard through a stethoscope will usually be rasping and noisy from the windpipe, the sides of the neck will be swollen and temperature may be raised. Even after symptoms have subsided, dogs can remain infectious for up to three months.

In the US, the parainfluenza virus has been shown to be the main infectious agent involved, but in the UK, Glasgow Veterinary School showed that *Bordetella bronchiseptica*, a bacterium rather than a virus, was the main cause of so-called 'kennel cough'.

Your vet will advise you on the best method of treatment, depending on age, health and degree of the cough.

RABIES

With the current strict quarantine laws the UK is rabies-free and rabies

Ital. Int. Ch. Iulius Tocanen Ch'am Pias, bred and owned by Giulio Audisio di Somma.

Photo: Visintini.

vaccination is not usually carried out unless the animal is intended for export. In many countries of the world puppies need their rabies shots at about the same time as their other inoculations.

COMMON CONDITIONS

ITCHY SKIN
Airedales sometimes suffer from skin problems but not as much as other breeds. If your pet is constantly scratching, there are many reasons after fleas have been ruled out. Try changing his diet and monitor him for three or four weeks. Feed a low-protein food, such as complete chicken and rice, one of many on the market.

If you use a flea spray or flea-repellent drops administered to the top of the shoulder, it could be that your dog is among those allergic to many types of flea repellents. Try avoiding conventional drugs.

Some animals can be allergic to grass but very rarely does this occur in an Airedale.

ANAL GLANDS
There are two of these in the dog, situated slightly below and to each side of the anus. These ducts produce a fluid and may become blocked so the secretions cannot escape and the glands swell. Sometimes there is infection and the normal secretion is replaced by a brownish, foul-smelling pus. Irritation or pain then results. Symptoms include yelping, constant sitting down, and tail-chasing; your Airedale may drag his rear end on the ground or carry his tail low.

Empty the glands by folding a few layers of kitchen roll, placing it over the anus, and applying pressure to the glands (if enlarged they can be easily felt) with a finger and thumb on either side of the anus. If the glands are waxy and difficult to expel or spots of blood appear or the dog suffers pain, seek veterinary help.

HEAT STROKE
Hot weather can be dangerous for any dog – at such times take your Airedale out for walks in the early morning or late at night. Never shut your pet in a hot room in the summer and never leave him in a car while you go shopping! Heat kills. If you find yourself in an emergency situation, treatment must be quick in order to be effective. The body temperature has to be lowered. Take the animal to water immediately and wet all his body or use ice packs to reduce his body heat. The time required to bring down the temperature should be around ten to 15 minutes. Seek veterinary help if this is not the case.

CHOCOLATE AND DOGS
Highly toxic to dogs is a constituent of chocolate called theobromine – dark cooking chocolate contains the most. The effect is dependent on the amount he has ingested. One dog may only suffer slight diarrhoea, but it could trigger cardiac irregularity or epileptic fits in others. The best policy is to avoid giving your pet any chocolate at all.

HIP DYSPLASIA – HD
Airedales are a medium-to-large breed and, like many large breeds, can have occurrences of hip dysplasia. Cases of HD are not common in Airedales, but the possibility should be addressed. Most breeders have their breeding stock hip-scored. The animal's hip joints are X-rayed by the vet and the film is then

sent to the Veterinary Association for evaluation. This helps breeders select good stock, and dogs that do not meet the hip requirement are not bred from.

The symptoms of HD are that, from an early age, the dog will not walk for long periods and he may seem to sit quite a lot or may have difficulty in rising from a sitting or prone position. Surgical options are available.

CONGENITAL EYE PROBLEMS

ENTROPION
The eyelid turns inwards, causing the lashes to dig into the surface of the eye. This can be painful for the animal, who will appear to be squinting and whose eye is red and very sore.

ECTROPION
The eyelids turn outwards. This causes tears to pool in the pouch formed by the lid and the cornea dries out.

TRICHIASIS
The dog's eyelashes may grow in the wrong direction so they rub on the eye and cause pain.

DISTICHIASIS
A similar problem, where extra hairs are on the edge of the lid and rub the eye.

All these eye problems, if left untreated, may cause serious damage, even blindness. If your animal suffers from any of the above conditions, it should not be included in your breeding programme. Fortunately for affected animals, surgery or electrolysis can remove the hairs.

FINALLY...
If in any doubt concerning the health of your pet after you have referred to this part of the book, may I suggest you take your pet to your veterinary surgery for a diagnosis.

6 *THE VERSATILE AIREDALE*

Many people do not appreciate the sporting capabilities of the Airedale, but in fact the breed is used for hunting and working in many parts of the world.

OBEDIENCE IN THE USA

American Airedales and their owners participate keenly in Obedience and Agility and compete enthusiastically in the show ring. A good introduction to Agility would be the Obedience ring. We have often seen the Airedale working in that arena, but not with the flash and enjoyment many of the other breeds exhibit. His independent nature and occasional stubborn attitude make him a challenge for even the greatest trainer. It can be a fine line trying to determine what he will do to please you, and what he will do to please himself. It takes a sense of humour to work alongside your Airedale, but, once the bond has been established, there is almost nothing that defeats him.

In the early 1980s, work was begun to form an Obedience committee to look at establishing a separate Obedience competition on the Montgomery County

Multi Ch. Tintara Much-Enough, bred by Pat Crome, owned by P. Hjelm.
The Airedale is an intelligent dog who is capable of taking on a variety of tasks.

weekend. Since there is nothing that an Airedale or his owner cannot do, after due process and much work, the trial was started, along with a separate Top Obedience Airedale Award and Top Novice Obedience Award. These represented a significant step in recognizing the efforts and hard work that Airedales and their trainers put in during the year. This independent Obedience trial helped to promote and encourage the effort and hard work of all Airedale owners. The first such award was made in 1988 to Covenay Bingley Barrister UD.

On reviewing the numbers of Obedience titles awarded, several interesting facts came to light. For every 40 or so Airedales registered, one becomes a breed Champion. For every 80 Airedales registered, only one will receive a CD (Companion Dog) title. One of every six CD Airedales will go on to achieve his CDX, and out of every six CDX Airedales, one will go on to achieve his UD (Utility Dog) title. That is approximately one UD title for every 1509 Airedales registered.

Since Airedale owners all know that beauty and brains do mix, statistics show that over half of the Obedience title holders were sired by Champions and more than a fair share had Champion dams.

Because of the popularity of the Obedience trials held at Specialty shows, more people are attending as spectators. Many of these spectators will be next year's exhibitors. Yes, we can say that Obedience is very much alive and well in America.

OBEDIENCE IN THE UK
by Angela Walters
Robroyd Lapis Lazuli (Mollie) was born in June 1994 and is a shining example of an Airedale who has responded well to Obedience training.

Her owner, Angela Walters, had owned two dogs previously – a Jack Russell Terrier dog named Ricky and a bitch called Tina, a German Shepherd cross. Angela lived alone and, when she lost Tina, she wanted a dog of medium size, one she could handle herself, who would be loyal, a good guard as well as friendly – no hair loss was also an advantage. She had fond memories of her grandmother's Airedale (Peggy, a volunteer police dog, but that is another story) and so Angela decided on the breed.

Mollie was from a litter of just three bitches, two of whom I had kept for myself. Their dam was Ch. Robroyd Emerald, Top Airedale bitch 1992, and the sire was Ch. Robroyd Granite.

Angela began simple training with Mollie from the beginning. Twelve weeks was a good age to leave her litter sisters, and moreover she had finished her course of vaccinations. She was ready to begin simple exercises and to socialise more.

The pair began attending a dog training club when Mollie was 16 weeks old in the beginners' class. Both her other dogs had attended dog training classes, so she had some previous experience, which helped. Mollie met Omar the yellow Labrador and his owner Shirley. Omar was only one day older than Mollie and, from that first meeting at the dog club to this day, all four remain very good friends. Shirley's sister, June, was also attending classes with her dog Dushka, a four-year-old black German Shepherd crossed with Labrador. Mollie loves Shirley and June and is excellent with Omar and Dushka.

The Pontefract Dog Training Team with Robroyd Lapis Lazuli (Mollie) and handler Angela Walters.

Such relationships are a huge bonus of training classes. Mollie had always been a friendly dog, mixing well with other dogs and people. Angela used to think she was too friendly at first but, now Mollie is a little older, she is learning not to trust everyone she meets.

Mollie was hard to train at first; terriers seem to have a mind of their own. Angela was told by fellow enthusiasts that Airedales can be hard to train, as they do not mature until around the age of three years. Mollie has been brought up with Omar and Dushka and they all go for walks and have intervals of training in between playtimes.

Sometimes, Shirley will swap Omar with for Mollie and she and Angela train each other's dog. The same applies when Dushka and June are training. They entered all three dogs in an Obedience class for beginners, for the experience. Mollie did quite well on two occasions, only losing one and a half points.

Mollie proved quite disobedient and difficult to train at first, being more interested in running off and playing with other dogs than in doing what she was told. With patience, and plenty of tidbits, Angela made progress.

Angela would also train Mollie at home, in the hall or the garden, depending on the weather. She taught her to Sit and Stay, walking around her while she was on the lead, then doing the same while she was in the Down

position, tugging at the lead but simultaneously telling her to "Stay".

To teach Mollie the Recall, she was told to sit (kept on the lead) then, taking one step back, Angela called her in, using a tidbit and guiding her with the lead. This was repeated taking two steps backwards, and, gradually, Angela kept increasing the distance, dispensing with the lead, and Mollie would come towards her when called.

When Angela wanted Mollie to Stay, she would hold her hand up in front of her and give her the command. Her heel work was good; Mollie never pulled on the lead, always walking by Angela's side.

These were the main goals Mollie achieved in the beginners' class. To sit, to go down, and to stay when commanded to do so, both in Sit and in Down position, to do the Recall and to walk to heel.

Angela joined a display team formed by the club despite the fact that Mollie and Omar were still young. The first Obedience display was held after only ten weeks of training. Mollie did not let the team down although she was only 18 months old. The second display included Agility. All the dogs were left in a Down position in the centre of the arena while the owner/handlers put together the course. Mollie did very well over all the jumps, through the tunnels and the stretch jump, though she did miss some of the weave poles. Angela was very pleased with her as it was her first time. Both Omar and Mollie had done well. Later that year both moved into the second class. (The Advanced is surely not far away!)

That Christmas, Mollie was chosen as the dog which had made the most progress in Obedience throughout the year. Early in 1996, Mollie gained her Good Citizen award, various charity work was undertaken by the Club and the team donated to Dogs for the Disabled.

At the time of writing, both Angela and Mollie are having to work harder in the second class to perfect what Mollie has already been taught. When told to sit, she has to sit straight and not in 'puppy sit'. On Recalls she has to come in straight and not at an angle and then sit correctly in front of Angela to finish, first walking behind her back. Angela had already trained Mollie at home to sit and to do the Finish, so she had no problems in class. When doing heel work, Angela is now expected to do the footwork properly, not just to train Mollie to walk at heel. Angela still finds it hard to concentrate on what she is doing with her feet as well as training Mollie to walk to heel.

THE EXERCISES

Retrieve: Mollie has now learnt to retrieve. Angela started by asking her to "Hold", placing the dumb-bell in her mouth. At first, no matter how she tried, Mollie would not keep hold of it and kept dropping it on the floor. Eventually, when she did hold it, Angela quickly took it from her, not giving her chance to drop it again. She gave Mollie a tidbit; thus Mollie learnt that, if she held it for a time, she would get a reward. Angela built up the distance by, firstly, placing the dumb-bell on the floor immediately in front of Mollie and telling her to "Hold". When she picked it up and held it a few seconds, Angela took it from her and gave a tidbit. She kept placing the dumb-bell a little further away each time until eventually she was able to throw the dumb-bell a distance for Mollie to fetch. After a while, when Mollie started bringing it back, Angela got the dog to sit in front of her and told her to "Hold". When Mollie had learnt this, Angela asked her to do the Finish, which, of course, she could do already. It has taken some time to put it all together, but now Mollie is coming on fine and with a little more training should soon be able to do a Retrieve properly.

Sendaway: The pair have been practising Sendaways for a number of weeks. The trainer puts four cones down to form a square and a toy is placed in the centre. Angela then takes Mollie to the other end of the hall, tells her to "Look" and points her head in the direction of the toy, and says "Away". As Mollie runs towards the toy, Angela follows her and when she is about to pick up the toy Angela commands her to go down. Mollie needs to do a lot more training on the Sendaway.

Scent Cloths: Angela's club has only just started to train dogs using scent cloths; therefore a lot more training is needed.

Down Stay, Sit Stay, Stand Stay and the 'A' Recall: Mollie is fine when doing Down stays, Sit stays and Stand stays. The dogs are left several minutes in any of the above positions and owners usually go out of the room where they cannot be seen. Mollie has no problem with this at all. She is also now doing 'A' Recalls.

SUMMING UP
I will let Angela have the last word on her experience of Obedience with an Airedale: "Both Mollie and I enjoy training sessions; it is something we can do together and has enabled Mollie to mix both with dogs and other people. I wanted a dog I could take anywhere, without any problems, and learning Obedience has been very good for Mollie. We hope to continue training sessions and eventually take part in future events.

"Since Mollie came to live with me I know I made the right choice in having an Airedale Terrier. She is everything I need in a dog: lovable, loyal, mischievous, comical, a great character and an excellent companion."

COMPETITIVE OBEDIENCE IN THE UK
by Murial Carrott.

My first Airedale was four years old when I began to train her for Competitive Obedience. The previous years had been purely pet obedience, but, after a while, we won out of Beginners. The lowest class I could enter with my next Airedale, Elly, was the Novice Class.

Airedales have to have a reason to do the exercises they are asked to do. I have always found them to be food-orientated, so a little treat as a reward helps a lot. You cannot force an Airedale to do anything. If you shout at them, or ask them nicely, the minute they are away from you they will stand and laugh at you as much as to say "Now what are you going to do

about it?". I have found that if you are firm and look pleasant, they will do as you ask within reason. At least, this was so with Elly. Until I realised this, we had a fight at every lesson and I became very frustrated and angry. I still have to be one step ahead of her because, if she thinks she can get away with anything, she will try it.

When Elly has learned an exercise one way, if you try to alter this, she stands and looks at you as much as to say "That's not right. That's not how we do it!". I remember in training classes tackling Distance Control (asking your dog to go into either the Sit, Down or Stand position). The last position on this occasion was the Stand and the trainer said, "Leave your dogs in this position while all the Working Trials dogs Speak on Command". I knew Elly could do this, so I said "Elly speak". Nothing happened. She just looked at me with a questioning expression. Again I said "Elly speak"; again, nothing, but this time she also looked at the trainer. It happened a third time. Eventually the trainer explained: "Elly has just said 'My mum is asking me to speak and we haven't finished off the last exercise." Sure enough, when I said "Elly Finish" and praised her, then asked her to speak, she did so, quite loudly too! I was absolutely amazed, but it taught me a lesson. Elly thinking for herself was one of the problems I had to work through in my Obedience work with her.

My other Airedale, Kaiya (Elly's daughter), is entirely different. She is so eager to please that sometimes she gets it all wrong and then gets very embarrassed. But she loves to play and tug the lead, so with her I put the control in as we play, and I have taught her that the word

"Working" means she has to get into the heel work position.

It really is a pleasure to work with her but I have to be careful about the tone of voice. If I am too severe, she gets sulky and her tail goes under.

People keep asking me "When are you going to change your breed of dog?". I reply "Not for all the tea in China". I know Airedales can be a little 'difficult' at times, but the pleasure of working with them, the fun, and the feeling of achievement at the end of the day is fantastic.

The Airedale is built for agility, and they seem to love the challenge offered by this sport. Tien Tran Photography.

AGILITY IN THE USA
Many Airedale owners have found an interest in the Agility ring. While it has long been a popular sport in England, it has only been an AKC-recognized event since the mid-1990s. Since then, its popularity has sky-rocketed. In 1996, the AKC recorded approximately 30,000 Agility entries. In 1997, that number more than doubled. Of course, that includes all breeds. It is easy to understand why the sport is growing so rapidly since it is such great fun for the handler and the dog. It affords an opportunity to spend quality fun time with your dog. Agility proves a perfect opportunity for combining dog shows and real fun, working as a team with your dog and competing, yet thoroughly enjoying the breathtaking run.

Agility seems to be designed for Airedales – nothing is the same two times in a row – and a sense of humour is a prerequisite for entry into the ring. Agility seems to combine the interest of Obedience along with the fun of running a course filled with differing challenges. From the weave poles to the jumps and tunnels, the Airedale can assume his

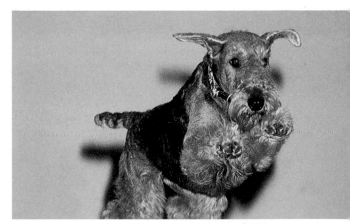

Am. Ch. Spindletop's Best Of My Love tackling the obstacles (and below). Critter Pictures.

Critter Pictures.

independent air and still have fun. Airedales seem to be more deliberate than the more popular Agility breeds, the Border Collies and Shelties. One can almost see them exercise their thoughts on how the course should be run.

Currently the Airedale Terrier Club of America has several members that are active in the sport and expects that number to grow as Agility becomes even more popular. Currently plans are afoot to prepare for holding Agility trials at the majority of National Specialties, including the Montgomery County Kennel Club weekend.

AGILITY IN THE UK
by Jane Turner (Crillee Airedales)

Firstly, and most importantly, your Airedale must be fit and healthy. It is also important to have total control at all times; he must be able to listen to you and obey familiar but simple commands such as "Sit", "Wait", "Down", "Come", etc. That may seem fairly straightforward if you have a working breed such as a Border Collie, but most terriers are quite independent and conveniently go 'deaf', especially if there is something more interesting on the other side of the fence.

The Airedale Terrier is a great crowd-puller; he loves to clown around and show off to an audience – which is why he will usually do the most unexpected thing at a time when you least welcome it. A typical example of this is an Airedale male who was a real exhibitionist in Agility. He knew how to tackle all the obstacles and was a real 'pro'. When performing in front of a large crowd, he would start enthusiastically but, as soon as he approached the A-frame, his personality would change. He would run

up the A-frame to the top, then stop, for what seemed a lifetime to his handler, survey all around him, and bark several times just to get the crowd's full attention. He would then proceed down the other side, make a bee-line for the tunnel ignoring his handler's frustrated cries, charge through the tunnel, stop at the other end just inside the tunnel, sniff its outer rim and then, with a wicked smile, would cock his leg against the wall of the tunnel. His handler was left blushing with embarrassment. The crowd loved it – and so did the Airedale.

This kind of behaviour is very typical of the breed and can be frustrating for the handler, so you must realise the importance of being in control. If you love a challenge in Agility, then the Airedale will certainly give you one.

The first thing on the agenda is to join a good training club, one that can offer both Obedience and Agility. When enrolling, inform them of your intention to learn Agility with your Airedale. In an ideal world, you will know this when your Airedale is a puppy and you can begin with basic Obedience and work towards Agility when you have the desired control – but only when your Airedale is mature enough. Remember, *never* jump your Airedale puppy over obstacles, as this could lead to joint problems later in life. Work a step at a time and do not 'run before you can walk'.

Most dogs learn by repetition and, if you have a large garden, it is worth purchasing some Agility equipment or making a few items so you can practise every day. This is the ideal way to get the dog to learn quicker.

Never force your Airedale over obstacles; rather, encourage him, gain his confidence and give him lots of praise along with the correct command on approach. Each obstacle must be taught separately as they are all very different.

At the beginning, always train on the lead, assisting your dog over each obstacle and making sure the instructor is on the other side of your Airedale helping him to keep his balance. Most good Agility clubs will have half-scale obstacles which are designed for beginners and are less intimidating on the approach.

You can teach your Airedale puppy the basics of Agility. There are many contact obstacles which do not entail any jumping, a few of which are the A-frame, the seesaw and the dog walk. Other obstacles which can be fun when teaching your puppy are the collapsible tunnel and the weaving poles. The tunnel can be especially good fun to teach, potentially involving handler participation (in the form of crawling through the tunnel, though this is not compulsory). Better still, the correct way to teach your Airedale to go through the tunnel is with the help of your instructor who will hold on to your dog at the entrance to the tunnel while you as the handler proceed to the other end and call your Airedale by name, making sure he can see you through the tunnel. The instructor will encourage him to enter the tunnel while you call him by name at the other end, praising him as he comes through and also when he is out.

All dog training clubs have different methods of teaching Agility and each instructor will use different techniques. Some breeds (and humans) learn quicker than others and every instructor should be sympathetic to those who find it more difficult, although the basic principles are

the same. Approach obstacles giving the correct command – in the above instance, "Weave". The dog then executes the obstacle with encouragement from the handler and comes out or off the other end. Make sure the contact points are touched by the dog at the beginning and at the end; you may need to steady your dog at both these points.

Agility is a great hobby and will not only keep you and your Airedale fit, but will also keep his mind occupied. Like many other breeds, Airedales can be destructive when bored. The Airedale is a very intelligent breed – read his moods, stay one step ahead of him, and you will gain his respect. Above all, never lose your temper, as it will only make matters worse. To get the best out of an Airedale, nothing replaces praise and reward.

THE WORKING DOG IN THE US

Since all Airedale owners realize how truly unique the breed is, many fanciers have taken this dog back to his original purpose and have developed a hunting and working trial to use his skills.

Through the efforts of Steve and Bonnie Gilbert of Ohio and many other dedicated Airedale owners, the first national Airedale workshop for hunting and working events was held in 1986. This annual event developed performance standards and the tests necessary to gain support not only among Airedale people, but also to receive the imminent recognition of the American Kennel Club; for it is hoped that these tests will soon be recognized as an American Kennel Club approved event.

To receive the recognition of AKC, the Airedale Terrier Club of America

A hunting workshop for Airedales met with an enthusiastic response.

through its Hunting and Working committee started to sponsor hunting tests in 1994. Tests are now offered at Junior, Senior and Master levels.

In the Upland Bird test, Airedales are required to find and flush two planted birds and do one water retrieve. Qualifying dogs receive the Junior Hunter-Flushing certificate. Greater proficiency must be demonstrated to complete the Senior Hunter and Master Hunter titles.

In the Retrieving test, a dog must retrieve two chukars on land and two ducks on water. Qualifying awards are offered in all three levels, Junior, Senior and Master.

In the Fur test a dog must follow a pre-laid track of raccoon scent on an indirect

Am. Ch. Moraine Prime Minister showing the natural retrieving skills required in Hunting Tests.

Photo: Chris Halvorson.

route through fields to a tree holding a caged raccoon. The dog must then bark or bay to announce the find. More difficult tracks are necessary to advance to Senior and Master awards.

The dog that qualifies in all three basic tests receives the title Junior Hunter-Versatile. Senior Hunter-Versatile and Master Hunter-Versatile are further possibilities. These tests provide further proof that Airedales have extraordinary talents and are capable of still serving the purpose for which they were originally bred.

THE WORKING GUN DOG
by Margaret Kirby

Near Scarborough, in Yorkshire, a Barnsley-bred bitch, Coomboots Amber Penny (affectionately known as Penny), believes that she is a working gun dog, rather than an Airedale Terrier.

Brought up in the country home of Colin and Margaret Kirby, Penny had her early training with Margaret at an all-breeds dog training club where she gained her Police Obedience Road-training Elementary and Intermediate Awards with Excellence by her first birthday. Penny twice won a Novice Obedience Class for Heel on-lead, Heel off-lead, Recall, Sit and stay and Down and stay.

During the next winter, Penny accompanied her master pheasant shooting and gained quite a reputation for seeking lost birds and retrieving them. The following summer, Colin took on the role of part-time gamekeeper for his shoot. When the pheasants arrived, Penny accompanied her master and quickly learned to gently round up the young chicks, rather like a

Coomboots Amber: A great working gundog, with her owner, Colin Kirby.

sheepdog with a flock of sheep, guiding them back into their pen twice a day for feeding and for safety. This continued all summer. Penny knew just what to do without being told. Despite retrieving game each winter, she never hurt a chick.

Occasionally, for no known reason, pheasants take fright and fly to the ground. When this happened, Penny would instantly lie flat to the ground, blending beautifully with the surrounding bracken and brambles, allowing the birds to settle around her. Penny was permitted to attend the local shoot's summer working days. Everyone knew she would stay where left and

In Italy, Iulius Intrepid has been trained to retrieve game.
Bred by Audisio di Somma, owned by Marco Lenuzza.
Photos: Marco Lenuzza.

never think to wander off into the woods to hunt on her own, even when a wandering cock pheasant approached her and shouted his annoyance.

Throughout her nine working years as a gun dog, she would often be put into cover when a pheasant was lost and the other gun dogs were unable to find the bird. More often than not, Penny would come out with the bird in her mouth! On one occasion she had to be guided back by voice alone – the pheasant's wing was completely across her face and eyes – but with faith in her master's voice, the bird was brought back to his feet.

Penny died this year, but has left many enduring memories. The Scarborough & District All Breeds Dog Club awarded her 'The Best Retrieve of the Year' in a final tribute to a remarkable dog who was still working the year she died.

Penny's 'tricks' included carrying raw eggs gently in her mouth and collecting the post and newspaper. She loved to exercise with a horse. The Kirbys' daughter, Susan, qualified for the British Riding Club's National Finals for Show Jumping and also entered the Horse and Hound Class. Horses and riders jump half-a-dozen fences, then dismount and swap horse for dog and complete a small obstacle course (jumps, tyres and weaving through bending poles). Penny was the only Airedale taking part and did not disgrace the trio with one of the fastest times of the day.

Colin is now training his third Airedale gun dog, Dendaric Merlindos Cognac (Chloe to her friends). In 1996, Chloe gained her Kennel Club Good Citizen award. She was bred by David and Denise Brown (Dendaric), both of whom are Championship-level judges.

7 *THE BREED STANDARDS*

What is A Breed Standard? To answer this question, it is helpful to quote directly from the UK Kennel Club's own publication *Illustrated Breed Standards:*

"Each breed has a descriptive Standard – a word picture or specification – which details its essential features. The Standards have recently been revised with the objects, first, of removing descriptions deleterious to the wellbeing of the dogs, and, second, of setting out the salient features in a logical and consistent sequence. These Standards are accepted by many overseas kennel Authorities as the definitive statements on the breeds..."

THE UK AIREDALE TERRIER BREED STANDARD
Printed by kind permission of The Kennel Club.

GENERAL APPEARANCE
Largest of the Terriers, a muscular, active, fairly cobby dog, without suspicion of legginess or undue length of body.

CHARACTERISTICS
Keen of expression, quick of movement, on the tip-toe of expectation at any movement. Character denoted and shown by expression of eyes, and by carriage of ears and erect tail.

TEMPERAMENT
Outgoing and confident, friendly, courageous and intelligent. Alert at all times, not aggressive but fearless.

HEAD AND SKULL
Skull long and flat, not too broad between ears, and narrowing slightly to eyes. Well balanced, with no apparent difference in length between skull and foreface. Free from wrinkles, with stop hardly visible, cheeks level and free from fullness. Foreface well filled up before eyes, not dishfaced or falling away quickly below eyes, but a delicate chiselling prevents appearance of wedginess or plainness. Upper and lower jaws deep, powerful, strong and muscular, as strength of foreface is greatly desired. No excess development of the jaws to give a

Ch. Karudon Kornilla: Top Airedale bitch in the UK 1999. Bred by Ruth Millar.
A very feminine Airedale, yet with plenty of substance. She has excellent legs and feet, and has the correct powerful movement.

rounded or bulging appearance to the cheeks, as 'cheekiness' is undesirable. Lips tight, nose black.

EYES
Dark in colour, small, not prominent, full of terrier expression, keenness and intelligence. Light or bold eyes highly undesirable.

EARS
'V' shaped with side carriage, small but not out of proportion to size of dog. Top line of folded ear slightly above level of skull. Pendulous ears or ears too high undesirable.

MOUTH
Teeth strong. Jaws strong. Scissor bite, i.e. upper teeth closely overlapping the lower teeth and set square to the jaws, preferable, but vice-like bite acceptable. An overshot or undershot mouth undesirable.

NECK
Clean, muscular, of moderate length and thickness, gradually widening towards shoulders and free from throatiness.

FOREQUARTERS
Shoulders long, well laid back, sloping obliquely, shoulder blades flat. Forelegs perfectly straight with good bone. Elbows perpendicular to body, working free of sides.

BODY
Back short, strong, straight and level, showing no slackness. Loins muscular. Ribs well sprung. In short-coupled and well ribbed-up dogs there is little space between ribs and hips. When a dog is long in couplings some slackness will be shown here. Chest deep (i.e. approximately level with elbows), but not broad.

HINDQUARTERS
Thighs long and powerful with muscular second thigh, stifles well bent, turned neither in or out. Hocks well let down, parallel with each other when viewed from behind.

FEET
Small, round and compact, with good depth of pad, well cushioned, and toes moderately arched, turning neither in nor out.

TAIL
Set on high and carried gaily, not curled over back. Good strength and substance. Customarily docked. Tip approximately at same height as top of skull.

Ch. Saredon Handyman: The UK's male breed recordholder with 32 CCs, and a Group winner.
Bred by Judy Averis and David Scawthorne.

GAIT/MOVEMENT

Legs carried straight forward. Forelegs move freely parallel to the sides. When approaching, forelegs should form a continuation of the straight line in front, feet being same distance apart as elbows. Propulsive power is furnished by hind legs.

COAT

Hard, dense, wiry, not so long as to appear ragged. Lying straight and close, covering body and legs, outer coat hard, wiry and stiff, undercoat shorter and softer. Hardest coats are crinkling or just slightly waved; curly or soft coat highly undesirable.

COLOUR

Body saddle black or grizzle as top of the neck and top surface of the tail. All other parts tan. Ears often darker tan, and shading may occur round neck and side of skull. A few white hairs between forelegs acceptable.

SIZE

Height about 58-61 cms (23-24 ins) for dogs, taken from top of shoulder, and bitches about 56-59 cms (22-23 ins).

FAULTS

Any departure from the foregoing points should be considered a fault and the seriousness with which the fault should be regarded, should be in exact proportion to its degree.

Note: Male animals should have two apparently normal testicles fully descended into the scrotum.

THE AMERICAN BREED STANDARD

(Adapted by the Airedale Terrier Club of America. Approved by the Board of Directors of the American Kennel Club, July 14, 1959, and accepted as of this date.)

HEAD

Should be well balanced with little apparent difference between the length of skull and foreface.

SKULL

Should be long and flat, not too broad between the ears and narrowing very slightly to the eyes. Scalp should be free of wrinkles, stop hardly visible and cheeks level and free from fullness.

EARS

Should be V-shaped with carriage rather to the side of the head, not pointing to the eyes, small but not out of proportion to the size of the dog.

Am. Ch. Serendipity's Eagle's Wings: Top Airedale in the US 1994-1996, and top Airedale sire for 1997.
A wonderful dog to show; up on leg, great coat, short back and perfect tail-set. A beautiful head and ears, and a fluid mover.

The top line of the folded ear should be above the level of the skull.

FOREFACE
Should be deep, powerful, strong and muscular. Should be well filled up before the eyes.

EYES
Should be dark, small, not prominent, full of terrier expression, keenness and intelligence.

LIPS
Should be tight.

NOSE
Should be black and not too small.

TEETH
Should be strong and white, free from discoloration or defect. Bite either level or vice-like. An overlapping or scissor bite is permissible without preference.

NECK
Should be of moderate length and thickness gradually widening toward the shoulders. Skin tight, not loose.

SHOULDERS AND CHEST
Shoulders long and sloping well into back. Shoulder blades flat. From the front, chest deep but not broad. The depth of the chest should be approximately on a level with the elbows.

BODY
Back should be short, strong and level. Ribs well sprung. Loins muscular and of good width. There should be but little space between the last rib and the hip-joint.

HINDQUARTERS
Should be strong and muscular with no droop.

TAIL
The root of the tail should be set well up on the back. It should be carried gaily but not curled over the back. It should be of good strength and substance and of fair length.

LEGS
Forelegs should be perfectly straight, with plenty of muscle and bone.

ELBOWS
Should be perpendicular to the body, working free of sides.

THIGHS
Should be long and powerful with muscular second thigh, stifles well bent, but not turned either in or out, hocks well let down, parallel with each other when viewed from behind.

FEET
Should be small, round and compact, with a good depth of pad, well cushioned; the toes moderately arched, not turned either in or out.

COAT
Should be hard, dense and wiry, lying straight and close, covering the dog well over the body and legs. Some of the hardest are crinkling or just slightly waved. At the base of the hard, very stiff hair should be a shorter growth of softer hair termed the undercoat.

COLOR
The head and ears should be tan, the ears being of a darker shade than the rest. Dark markings on either side of the skull are permissible. The legs up to the thighs and elbows and the under part of the body and chest are also tan and the tan frequently runs into the shoulder. The sides and upper part of the body should be black or dark grizzle. A red mixture is often found in the black and is not to be considered objectionable. A small white blaze on the chest is a characteristic of certain strains of the breed.

SIZE
Dogs should measure approximately 23 inches in height at the shoulder, bitches slightly less. Both sexes should be sturdy, well muscled and boned.

MOVEMENT
Movement or action is the crucial test of conformation. Movement should be free. As seen from the front, the forelegs should swing perpendicular from the body free from the sides, the feet the same distance apart as the elbows. As seen from the rear the hind legs should be parallel with each other, neither too close nor too far apart, but so placed as to give a strong well-balanced stance and movement. The toes should not be turned either in or out.

FAULTS
Yellow eyes, hound ears, white feet, soft coat, being much over or under the size limit, being undershot or overshot, having poor movement, are faults which should be severely penalised.

The use of any and all foreign agents for the improvement of dogs in the show ring, such as coloring, dilating the pupil and stiffening the coat, is forbidden under American Kennel Club rules; such acts are unsportsmanlike and unfair to those exhibitors who live up to the rules.

71

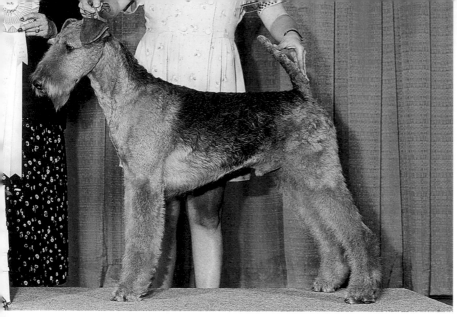

Can. Ch. Blue Jay of Paradym (Am. Can. Ch. Serendipity's Eagle's Wings – Am. Can. Ch. Paradym So Surreal).

SCALE OF POINTS

Head	10
Neck, Shoulders and Chest	10
Body	10
Hindquarters and Tail	10
Legs and Feet	10
Coat	10
Color	5
Size	10
Movement	10
General Characteristics and Expression	15
Total	100

Printed by kind permission of The American Kennel Club.

THE CANADIAN BREED STANDARD

The Airedale Breed Standard as set out by the Canadian Kennel Club (CKC) parallels the English and American Breed Standards. Conformation, temperament and type essentially remain the same; only the wording is slightly different. However, in Canada and the USA, the size is 23 ins height at the shoulder for dogs, with bitches slightly less, whereas, in England, about 23-24 ins for dogs and about 22-23 ins for bitches is stipulated.

In Canada and the USA the bite is either level or vice-like. A slightly overlapping or scissor bite is permissible without preference. Teeth must be white and free from discoloration or defect. In England, the scissor bite is stipulated with a vice-like bite acceptable. The scale of points for conformation is identical in Canada and the USA.

INTERPRETATION OF THE STANDARDS

There should be nothing overdone or out of balance in a winning Airedale. He has not strayed away from the Standard with exaggeration, as some terriers seem to have done.

GENERAL APPEARANCE

The factors which impress to the greatest degree are those of balance, size and substance, strength, temperament, activity and power. No single point outweighs any other in the overall picture. He should present an impressive all-round balance with type and character – after all, is he not the King of Terriers?

The Airedale is a relatively squarely built animal, and he is balanced; the length of body from point of shoulder to stern should be equal to the distance from withers to foot. He should cover plenty of ground with a long forehand and still have a short back, so there is a general impression of compactness, together with activity and speed. There should be no undue length or slackness in any part.

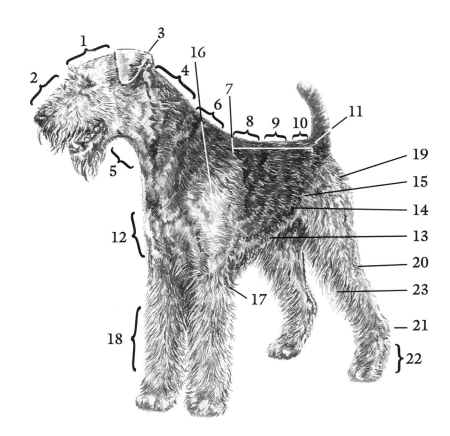

1. Forehead	9. Lumbar region	17. Elbow
2. Foreface	10. Croup	18. Forearm
3. Occiput	11. Set on	19. First thigh
4. Crest of neck	12. Brisket	20. Second thigh
5. Throat	13. Loin	21. Hock
6. Withers	14. Chest wall	22. Pastern
7. Line of back	15. Flank	23. Stifle
8. Dorsal region	16. Shoulder	

Correct proportions of the head, viewed in profile.

Incorrect: The foreface is short, the stop is pronounced, the cheeks are not level, and the dog is too throaty.

Correct: A typical male head, viewed from the front.

This head would be correct for a bitch; it would be acceptable in a juvenile male, but would be considered too narrow for a mature male.

Incorrect: Domed skull.

Incorrect: Broad skull.

THE HEAD

The head is long and strong, and brick-shaped, i.e. the foreface is the same length as the skull. Some kennels are straying away from this feature and their dogs have more length of muzzle. There should be little or no stop.

The skull and foreface should be on the same plane, with no suggestion of downface, as we sometimes see. Between the ears there should be good width; too little gives an impression of weakness,

DENTITION

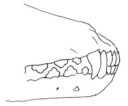

Correct:
Scissor bite.

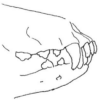

Incorrect:
Overshot.

Incorrect.
Undershot.

Acceptable:
Vice/level bite.

while too much can be described as a coarse-looking expression. Cheeks should be flat but well developed. The foreface tapers very slightly towards the nose but must be well filled before the eyes. The muzzle should have great strength.

MOUTH AND TEETH

The upper and lower jaw must be deep and wide with strong white teeth. The Standards call for a scissor bite with a level/vice-like bite being accepted. This is called a 'good mouth'. When either jaw is not correct, being over- or undershot, it can be seen easily by the placement of the canine teeth. A distinct space between the upper and lower canine teeth, showing that the lower teeth are well ahead of the upper, means that the jaw is what is usually termed undershot. The worst is overshot, and the overlapping upper teeth can to a degree hide the fault of a less than strong jaw. However, a dog with a perfectly strong upper and lower jaw with canines meeting tightly with level bite can be condemned by some judges, who prefer a scissor bite.

EYES

The eyes should be small to medium, dark (nearly black), with a 'varmint' expression and oval, not round, in shape. One article, commenting on eye colour, asked why, as long as a dog can see, should the colour of the eyes matter? But terrier folk know that an Airedale does not have the same expression with a light eye. It dilutes the hard-bitten look.

EARS

Ears are V-shaped and folded just above the top of the head, held alert with the points lying close. They should not be 'houndy' or overlarge.

THE EYES

Correct eye-shape and expression.

Incorrect: Large eyes.

THE EARS

Correct V-shaped ears.   *Incorrect: Hound ears.*

Incorrect: Flying ears.   *Incorrect: Button ears.*

THE NECK
A moderately long, well-arched neck is called for, flowing into sloping shoulders. A clean neck with no throatiness (loose skin) is what we should aim for. In profile, the neck should be neat and widening towards the shoulder, strong, well muscled, with the head carried high and proud.

THE FOREQUARTERS
The shoulders should slope, and be well laid back, flat and clean. The upper arm is short and steep, bringing the elbow well forward on the rib-cage. Viewed in profile, the dog shows little or no forechest and displays a clean line through from neck to feet.

THE FOREQUARTERS

Correct.   *Incorrect: Too narrow.*   *Incorrect: Too wide.*   *Incorrect: Turned out feet.*

Incorrect: Toed in.   *Incorrect: Out at elbow.*   *Incorrect: Base wide.*

The elbows should be held closely to the chest and defined, but should be capable of free movement forwards and backwards. The forelegs must be straight when viewed from any angle, well boned, with good furnishings. Pasterns should be short and upright, feet round and deep with strong pads, and toes moderately arched and tight together.

THE BODY
A short back is the desired quality in an Airedale but not too short, as this brings the risk of the shoulder being placed too far forward, which in turn restricts the length of stride, causing the dog to lose activity and waste energy. Some have said it restricts the ability to twist and turn rapidly, but I have not found this to be

true. Many people who work their Airedales do not like them too short in back. I agree that, when endurance and speed are the factors, more loin means the dog is far more supple for working tasks.

Ribs should be well sprung and deep to the elbow. Dogs with too much spring of rib may turn out at the elbows. So a happy medium is called for. The depth of the ribs in a mature dog should reach the elbows. Ribs should be carried well back, leaving little space between the end of the last rib and the hip joint, hence the term 'well ribbed up'. The loin is short and muscular and very slightly arched, to give strength in the area where it is most necessary, so a little less trimming to this area gives the desired level topline. When viewed from the front, the chest should be deep but not broad, the forelegs straight and parallel.

THE HINDQUARTERS

The croup is quite flat and the tail, customarily docked, rises up at a right angle with the last third sometimes turning towards the head ('tail set on top'). If the croup is too long, the tail will appear to be 'set-on' behind the dog. If the croup slopes down, the tail will appear low-set. The Airedale must have the correct type of croup, and a strong level topline is a major feature; anything that detracts from this is a very noticeable fault. This can be seen when the dog is viewed in motion from the side.

Seen both from the side and from behind, there should be good width across the thighs, with well-developed muscle in both first and second thighs. This part of the body has been called the dog's 'engine'. The first and second thigh should be fairly long, well bent at

THE BODY

Correct body proportions.

Incorrect: Too long in the back.

Incorrect: Shallow chest, straight stifle.

the stifle and hock, to give freedom of action with long strides.

The hocks should be close to the ground. When the dog is in motion or standing, they should be neither too close nor too far apart. The length of the hock usually determines the width of the stance. When the points of hock touch each other inwardly, this is called 'cow-hocked' and often means the dog is deficient in muscle tone. 'Open hock' means the opposite, that the hocks open outwardly. Such dogs are usually over-muscled and the stifles and toes turn in. It may not be beautiful, but it is at least an indication of strength. When viewed from the side, the point of the hocks should be – just – behind a vertical line drawn through the point of the buttocks.

MOVEMENT

The construction of the Airedale, with its short upper forearm, causes some of the breed to pick up their forelegs in the manner of the hackney horse. This is incorrect and wastes energy. The Airedale should take long, low strides in front, described by some as 'cutting the daisies'.

The hindquarters in the correct gait will show enough of the back pads, as the Airedale moves away, to show they are lifting true and equal with the hocks and displaying sufficient space between to show drive.

When viewed from the side, one should see a good topline, the forelegs showing good length of stride with a minimum of lift. The hindlegs should move with drive and purpose, co-ordinating with the front movement, neck slightly outstretched – bringing 'poetry in motion' to the onlooker.

THE HINDQUARTERS

Correct.

Incorrect. Too close behind.

Incorrect: Open hocks.

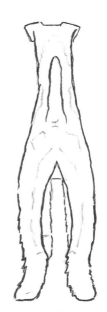

Incorrect: Cow hocks.

The correct Airedale gait, showing long, low strides.

Incorrect: Low tail-set, drooping croup.

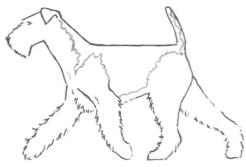

Incorrect: Straight shoulder.

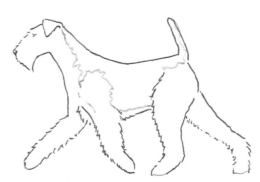

Incorrect: Dipped back, topline at an angle.

Incorrect: Roach back.

Incorrect: Pace movement.

Incorrect: Hackney movement.

Incorrect: Goose-stepping.

COAT

The Airedale's coat is a 'double' coat, the topcoat being hard, dense and wiry and the undercoat shorter and soft. Ideally, the coat should lie close and flat, though the hardest coats are crinkling or slightly waved. Soft or curly coats are undesirable. The Airedale is a beautiful dog and some faults will not look as obvious with clever presentation.

COLOUR

The colour of the coat should be black or black/grizzle. The legs up to the thighs and elbows, and the under part of the body and chest are tan. The tan colour also feathers a little into the shoulder. The ears are a darker shade of tan than the rest. Dark marks are acceptable each side of the skull and the neck. A few white hairs between the forelegs is acceptable.

SIZE

Males should measure 23-24 ins (58-61 cms) at the shoulder and should have two apparently normal testicles, while bitches measure 22-23 ins (56-59 cms). Bitches must retain femininity, no matter what their size, and a dog must always look masculine. Fashions in size can change from season to season, but an Airedale should look like the 'King of Terriers', without any undue coarseness. It is sad when a good specimen comes into the ring 'on size' and the other exhibits are small. Some argue that small dogs should be 'retired'. My own view is that each size can add to any breeding programme if they are sound.

TEMPERAMENT

Finally, temperament should be a vital factor – after all, this is what puts this breed above others. A typical Airedale has a kind and sensible nature but can show the terrier spirit. He can, if put to the test, hold his own should another dog engage him in any confrontation. This breed is an all-rounder, a worker in the field, a guard, a hunter, a family pet with humour to match the best. He is the perfect canine friend.

8 THE SHOW SCENE

INTRODUCTION FOR THE NOVICE

Showing can be a great hobby, and you should always accept it as just that. By all means, go out to win, but enjoy the sport, learn to accept your placing graciously, be kind to all the others and never forget to congratulate the winners. Pride in possessing something better than your neighbour has always been a failing of human nature, and nowhere has our ego been more evident than in showing dogs. That said, I believe that fair competition is healthy and harmless.

There is a negative side for those who like their sleep – most shows entail an early-morning journey to be there on time! Travel can be expensive, and so too can the entry fees – add it all up and showing Airedales can become a costly adventure. Most who attend the big shows have become ardent, dedicated exhibitors who thoroughly enjoy the day out, when they meet friends from all corners of the globe. This could be you in time!

Janet Huxley in the ring with Robroyd Lignum. Photo: Ted Stuart.

TRAINING FOR YOU AND YOUR PUPPY

Many clubs and canine societies hold monthly or weekly training sessions. Your national Kennel Club will assist you in finding the nearest club in your area.

These sessions are for all breeds and their aim is to assist the expert and teach the novice (whether the dog or the handler) in ring training. The venue is usually hired by the club and could be a church hall, social centre or even the local pub. Many people attend these sessions, some to train a young puppy, some to re-train an older dog, and the novice to learn how to train a dog. At these classes, you can also listen to feedback from people who have entered a dog or dogs at a recent show.

Training classes will teach your Airedale social habits and help him integrate with other animals. He will also become accustomed to having a stranger check his conformation. You will learn about different techniques used in the show ring. Social interaction of this sort gives both handler and dog a more confident and a happier approach when entering the show ring.

ENTRIES

When entering your first show you must apply for the schedule in advance. This can be awe-inspiring for any novice when you first read through it. The name of the dog must be exactly as is printed on the registration document. Seek the help of your breeder or someone who enters shows regularly to help you write in all the details. Note the closing date for entries and post your entry form, with the fee, to the secretary.

The age of your dog is the first important consideration when entering a class. You should not enter a puppy in the Open class. Read the 'Definitions of Classes' for that particular show in the schedule. This will help guide you through your entry details. Refrain from the impulse to enter too many classes when first exhibiting, sticking to two, e.g. puppy, and maybe novice if you and your dog are confident.

THE UK SHOW SYSTEM EXPLAINED

There follow the definitions of most of the classes found in many UK show schedules, although some shows may not provide all.

Minor Puppy: For dogs of six, and not exceeding nine, calendar months of age on the first day of the show.

In the UK, class allocations are decided on age, and what each dog has won.
Photo: Steph Holbrook.

Puppy: For dogs of six, and not exceeding twelve, calendar months of age on the first day of the show.

Junior: For dogs of six, and not exceeding eighteen, calendar months of age on the first day of the show.

Beginners: For owner, handler or exhibit not having won a first prize at a Championship or Open show.

Maiden: For dogs that have not won a Challenge Certificate or a first prize at an Open or Championship show (Minor Puppy, Special Minor Puppy, Puppy and Special Puppy classes excepted, whether restricted or not).

Novice: For dogs that have not won a Challenge Certificate (CC) or three or more first prizes at Open and Championship shows (Minor Puppy, Special Minor Puppy, Puppy and Special Puppy classes excepted, whether restricted or not).

Debutant: For dogs that have not won a CC or a first prize at a Championship show (Minor Puppy, Special Minor Puppy, Puppy and Special Puppy classes excepted, whether restricted or not).

Undergraduate: For dogs that have not won a CC or three or more first prizes at Championship shows (Minor Puppy, special Minor Puppy, Puppy and Special Puppy classes excepted, whether restricted or not).

Graduate: For dogs that have not won a CC or four or more first prizes at Championship shows in Graduate, Post Graduate, Minor Limit, Mid Limit,

Limit and Open classes, whether restricted or not.

Post Graduate: For dogs that have not won a CC or five or more first prizes at Championship shows in Post Graduate, Minor Limit, Mid Limit, Limit and Open classes, whether restricted or not.

Limit: For dogs that have not won three CCs under three different judges or seven or more first prizes in all, at Championship shows in Limit and Open classes.

Open: For all dogs, Champions included, of the breeds for which the class is provided and eligible for entry at the show.

Veteran: For dogs seven years or older on the first day of the show.

CHAMPIONSHIP SHOWS
All-Breed Championship Shows in the UK are usually held over a weekend, and some over two or three days, with individual breeds entering on certain days. This is where one can hopefully qualify for Crufts (only certain classes qualify) or try to gain a CC, as they are on offer for most of the breeds entered.

FIRST IN YOUR CLASS
If there are sufficient numbers in the ring, the judge will place first to fifth in each class. A red card for the winner, blue for second place and so on. (In America, blue cards are for first place winners and red for second).

From the unbeaten winners of each class there is the challenge (if you are lucky and win a first place, remember you have to be ready when the steward calls for all

unbeaten dogs). The judge then selects his best on the day from the line of winning dogs and awards a dog CC and a CC winner in bitches. Green cards signify these awards. The dog CC and bitch CC winners later meet together to determine the Best of Breed (BoB). There are also cards for the reserve CC (sometimes called reserve ticket winner) and they are for dog and bitch. They state that the dog or bitch is of sufficient merit to be worthy of being awarded the CC, if the CC winner were to be disqualified. The reserve CC is awarded to the second best dog and bitch in the breed. If the CC winner is disqualified, then the reserve CC winner becomes CC winner, though this very rarely happens.

The Best of Breed (BoB) is then entered in the Terrier Group. Here they challenge for Best Terrier in Group. In turn, the Group winner challenges the winners from the other six Groups for BIS (Best in Show).

Show results are published weekly in the two major dog papers and judges' critiques follow. To earn the title of Champion is no easy matter in the UK: the dog has to win three CCs under three different judges and one CC must be at over the age of twelve months. Competition is very intense when you

have won one or two CCs and are working for your third and final one.

There are a few Championship Shows which do offer CCs for all breeds (Crufts is one such show). A certain number of CCs are also allocated to breed club shows, our National Airedale Terrier Association being such a show. Many top Airedales are entered at such events and the competition is strong. Champions and CC winners compete with younger, up-and-coming Airedales for the roll of honour.

Championship Shows are open to all exhibitors and are the most important of all shows. They are also a good meeting point for anyone wanting to see the cream of the breed they are interested in. Meeting friends, many from overseas, is also one of the reasons for attending All-Breed Championship Shows.

Most all-breed clubs and breed clubs usually hold two or three shows a year and these types of shows are the ideal starting place for the novice. I began with the local shows and still attend them. The all-breed shows have smaller entries in the Airedale classes and, on some occasions, Airedale classes are not on offer and so you may enter 'Any Variety Terrier not separately classified'.

Usually the journeys to local shows are shorter and the entry fee is not expensive. You may glean much from watching the experienced exhibitor, observing all the trimmed breeds entered and mentally noting the preparations in hand just before the dogs walk into the ring. You can also observe the handling of the dogs in the ring. The different techniques used by various individuals may help you identify the best method of handling for you and your dog.

EXEMPTION AND SANCTION SHOWS

Exemption shows are open to registered and unregistered dogs. You can enter on the day of the show. This type of show is usually held to raise money for a charitable organisation. Fun classes are held, such as 'the most appealing eyes' the dog the judge would most like to take home', etc. A relaxed atmosphere is the order of the day. At sanction shows, you must be a member of the club to enter.

LIMIT SHOWS

Limit shows are also for club members only, and, again, there is a lovely relaxed atmosphere. No dog that has won a CC may enter.

OPEN SHOWS

Open Shows are, as the name suggests, open for all, Champions and novices alike. The dogs are allocated their own benches.

TERRIER SHOWS

One of my favourite shows of the year is the annual National Terrier Show. (Many people would choose otherwise, for example Crufts, Montgomery USA, Klub für Terrier in Germany, SIT

(Societa Italiana Terriers) in Italy, the World Show, etc.) The UK's National Terrier is an all-Terrier Championship Show held at Stafford, which is easily accessible. CCs are on offer for most of the Terrier breeds. Dog entries are high and the judges are sought-after experts in their own right. The show is, for me, the true Terrier day of the year, pleasantly set out, with dogs being the priority. Entry is free to the public and enthusiasts travel from the far corners of the British Isles and from abroad.

THE AMERICAN SYSTEM

The American system is in some ways very straightforward, but even so it has its complexities.

Whereas in Britain we have Championship shows, Open shows and Limited shows, most of the shows in the US are actually Points shows (Championship shows), though there are also "Match shows" which can be likened to the Open events in Britain. These are used by exhibitors mainly for accustoming young dogs to the show ring and are quite relaxed events.

Another point where the larger American shows and those in Britain and Europe differ is that in the US, many of the dogs are shown by professional handlers. Often a dog in the United States will be shown by its owner at smaller shows and breed specialties, but if it shows great promise it will be put in the hands of a professional handler who will travel great distances with it and campaign it far and wide. This can be an expensive business, and so inevitably breeders will be forced to find wealthy co-owners who will help finance their dog's show campaign. It is not unusual in the States to find dogs which have as

Am. Ch. Spindletop New Kid In Town: A top winning son of Am. Ch. Terrydale Int'l Affair. Photo: The Standard Image.

many as six co-owners, each of whom contributes to its campaign. Much expense is incurred with advertising the top-winning show dogs in countless specialist magazines, and this item alone can demand a budget of thousands of dollars per year.

BECOMING A CHAMPION

To become a Champion in the US requires the dog to win 15 points, including two "majors" (which must be of 3, 4 or 5 points) under at least three different judges. There are no age restrictions on a dog becoming an American Champion, and many "finish" their title as very young puppies.

The schedule of points in the US is quite complex. It is based on a mathematical formula that is applied to the actual dogs in competition within each sex of each breed, in each of the nine divisions in the continental US. It is calculated on a three-year basis.

The total number of shows where there was competition for a sex of a particular breed is taken, and the schedule for the following year is calculated so that as close as possible to 18 per cent of these

shows receive 3, 4 or 5 points. The entries at both specialty and all-breed shows are considered, although rotating national specialty shows are deleted from the calculation.

The projected schedule is based upon regular class competition only. Thus, if additional majors are created as a result of dogs going Best of Winners, Best of Breed or Best Opposite Sex, these are not considered in the calculations for future schedules.

There are so few shows in Alaska, Hawaii and Puerto Rico that these points schedules are calculated manually to ensure there are sufficient shows with majors.

No dog can win more than five points at any one show, but it is quite feasible for a dog to finish its title on three consecutive days, as many American shows are staged in clusters, with several shows being held in the same area over several consecutive days.

Once a dog has won its Championship title in the United States, it can then be automatically transferred into the Best of Breed class which is restricted to Champions. In essence, this means that the big difference between American shows and others is that a dog can win its Championship by beating only the non-Champions in its breed and sex, so it is obviously easier to become a Champion in the US than in Britain.

THE CLASSES

The classes which are on offer, prior to the Best of Breed class, for each sex are as follows:
Puppy – 6-9 months, or 6-12 months and 12-18 months – self-explanatory.
Novice – for dogs which have never won a blue ribbon (First) in any of the other

classes, or have won fewer than three ribbons in the Novice class.

Bred by Exhibitor – the exhibitor is also the breeder.

American-Bred – dog's parents mated in America and the dog was born in America.

Open – any dog of that breed.

After these classes are judged, all the dogs that won First place in the classes compete again to see who is the best of the winning dogs. This, too, is done separately for male and female dogs. Only the best male (Winners Dog) and the best female (Winners Bitch) receive Championship points. A Reserve Winner award is given in each sex to the Runner Up.

The Winners Dog and Winners Bitch then go on to compete with the Champions for the title of Best of Breed. Three awards are usually given:

Best of Breed – the dog judged as the best in its category.

Best of Winners – the dog judged best between the Winners Dog and Winners Bitch.

Best of Opposite Sex – the best dog that is the opposite sex to the Best of Breed winner.

Only the Best of Breed winners advance to compete in the group competition. The Bichon Frisé is classified in the Non-Sporting Group in the USA whereas in the UK it appears in the Toy Group. Again a point of confusion arises in the colours of American ribbons as opposed to British rosettes. In the UK, First Prize receives a red rosette (when they are offered), Second a blue, Third a yellow, and Reserve (fourth) a green. Fewer and fewer UK shows now offer rosettes, and it is not obligatory.

However, in the US ribbons must be awarded (when the judge feels the dogs merit it) as follows.

Blue:	For first place in any regular class. Also awarded to the winner of each group competition, usually in a rosette form.
Red:	For second place as above.
Yellow:	For third place as above.
White:	For fourth place as above.
Purple:	Awarded to the Winners Dog and Winners Bitch. Since these are the classes in which Championship points are earned, they are highly prized.
Purple and White:	Awarded to the Reserve Winners Dog and Reserve Winners Bitch.
Blue and White:	Awarded to the Best of Winners.
Purple and Gold:	Awarded to the Best of Breed.
Red and White:	Awarded to the Best of Opposite Sex.
Red, White and Blue:	Awarded only to the Best in Show.

THE FCI SYSTEM

The Fédération Cynologique Internationale, an umbrella organisation of which all the European countries, and many others, are members, suggests, for example, that dogs are first quality-graded and then those receiving the top

Japan: Airedale Terrier Club of Japan, Autumn Show.

grading compete for the placings in each of the classes. This can be confusing to foreign visitors as, when a Scandinavian exhibitor says that his dog has won a "First", this may mean simply a First grading (or Excellent if you happen to be in another country). This means that the dog is considered an excellent example of its breed with no serious faults. Those dogs which have obtained First gradings will then compete for the placings, and a further honour can be obtained if they receive a Certificate Quality grading.

Most of the FCI member countries also employ a system by which the judge gives each dog judged a detailed written critique, which is very helpful to the exhibitors, the breed clubs, and the judges themselves.

From the dogs graded Certificate Quality, the winners of the various certificates will be determined. This again may be confusing to the uninitiated, as it is not necessarily the best dog which receives the certificate! FCI rules dictate that dogs have to be of a certain age before they can win Certificates, and then when they have won so many, they can win no more; so it is quite feasible for, say, the dog standing Third in the Best Dog challenge to win an International Certificate, if the Best Dog is too young and the Second Best already has its International Title.

Finland: The Breeders Group at the Helsinki International Show. Pictured (left to right): Int. Ch. Big Lady's Monopolizer, Big Lady's Queen Regent, Int. Ch. Big Lady's Tina Turner, and Int. Ch. Big Lady's Magnetizer.

ITALY

The Italian Championship is quite different from the American. For Airedales, there are four classes: Young Class (from 6 to 9 months); Junior Class; Open Class (for the dogs at least 15 months old, the only class that gives the CAC), and the Champion Class.

Dogs can compete for the Championship in three different kinds of shows: International Shows, National Shows and Special Breed Shows.

In order to become a Champion in Italy, an Airedale must be classified 'Excellent 1st' in two Nationals, two Internationals and two Specials in the Open class (this means that it is sometimes easier to become an International Champion than an Italian Champion).

GERMANY

In Germany, there are approximately 45 Airedale shows a year. From these, you can obtain CC and reserve CC, besides junior CC and reserve junior CC. There are also International Shows where CACs (Certificate d'Aptitude au Championship) and CACIBs (Certificate d'Aptitude au Championship International de Beauté) can be won. For the title of German Champion a dog must gain four CCs, with one year between the first and the last, given by three different judges in at least three different federal states of Germany.

TRAVEL AND QUARANTINE

The British government has announced its intention to set up a pilot scheme – the so-called "pets' passport" to enable animals to travel to and from the UK. The scheme is set to run for a possible two-year period between Britain and other named rabies-free countries in the European Union.

This means that from April 2000, or possibly earlier, animals will be allowed to enter and leave Britain as long as they conform to strict vaccination, microchipping and blood-test regulations.

If the scheme is successful, it will be extended to ports other than those on the south coast, which, along with Heathrow airport, are the usual points of entry. Up-to-date information can be obtained from the UK Ministry of Agriculture, Fisheries and Food. It seems that the days of quarantine are at last numbered; no longer will animals travelling to our shores be routinely impounded.

SHOW PRESENTATION

Preparation for a show during the few days preceeding, it can be hectic if you are not working to a plan. Keep a calendar in your grooming area, or any place where you will always be able to note and stick to a plan of action.

You will have been working on the grooming of your dog for some weeks before the show. The dog may have his legs, underbody and facial beard bathed a few days before the show and the finishing touches such as feet and ears trimmed and cleaned.

Do not make the mistake of having to strip large areas of your Airedale's coat at the show. This should have been finished some days before. You may need to attend to certain areas of the coat, but the dog should not be worked on for long periods just before you enter your class, especially after a long journey.

A show should be an enjoyable experience for both dog and owner. If your Airedale is not prepared, it would

Italy: Multi Ch. Ginger Grappa, bred by Mrs A. Sommi-Picenardi.

Israel: Vullpet Aisqween, owned by Ilana Mashevski.

Sweden: Ch. Jokyl Extravaganza.

Russia: Rus. Ch. Strongfort Stirminator (Aust), bred by G. Lesh, owned by E. Lapina.

Holland: Multi Ch. Grace Of Malton.

Estonia: Multi Ch. Big Lady's Deedful Enough.

Belgium: Multi Ch. Miss Melody van't Asbroek.

Ireland: Ir. Ch. Bamhusa Scholar, bred and owned by Roy and Marion Gregg.

Australia: Aust. Grand Ch. Strongfort Solaris – to date, the only Grand Champion in the breed.

be better to miss the show than to take him looking untidy. All that should be required at the show in the way of final preparation is to work out the approximate time you will need to brush him up and comb his hair into place before he goes into the ring.

TRAVELLING IN GOOD TIME
You must look at your map and work out a timetable allowing for traffic problems, so that you do not enter the show ground at the last moment. Many exhibitors try to be there a couple of hours in advance, giving them time to exercise and settle the dogs and also (possibly) to have breakfast before the day begins! The journey must be pleasant and unhurried. The car is better loaded the night before with all the essentials. In the morning, all that is required is to exercise the dog or dogs and then settle them into the car for the journey.

Items you will need to take are:
Your dog passes (if you have entered a Championship Show). These are usually posted to you some time before the show, giving you and your dog entry into the show ground, with printed information as to your bench/exhibit number (also, if benching is compulsory, your benching area), the ring allocated to your breed and possibly the time of judging.
Dog crate (optional).
Dog blanket/rug.
Grooming table and grooming arm (in some countries, arms are not allowed).
Your grooming box.
A card clip – with which to attach your exhibiting number.
A small first aid box (this can be incorporated into your grooming box).
Dog bowls and water.

A towel – and lunch!

SHOW PROCEDURE
In the US and many other countries, benching is not used and exhibitors present themselves at the appropriate breed ring at the correct time. Hardworking ring stewards endeavour to make sure all competitors are in the ring at the correct time for their respective classes, but if the exhibitor misses his class he has only himself to blame.

If there is a Minor Puppy class (6-9 months of age), it will be the first class into the ring. This is not the best class for any exhibitor, the reason being that you have to be ready when the judge begins, as the steward then calls this class. This can cause a problem if a definite time has not been given, e.g. if another breed is judged before yours in your allocated ring. Do not panic if this happens – just ask one of the regular exhibitors when you arrive at the venue the approximate time that judging will commence.

You do not need to have your young puppy on the grooming table for too long a period. Watch the regular exhibitors – they would never tire a young dog by treating him in this way. The dog has to be fresh and alert. Try to work out from the catalogue how much time you will have available to prepare your Airedale for the class entered.

IN THE RING
It is important, if possible, to watch how the judge directs the ring before you enter it. This will give you advance notice of where he wants you all to stand, how he asks you to move your dog, and what he expects of you. Remember, if he asks for a triangle, do just that, not the sort of

Ch. Karudon Karlah, bred and owned by Ruth Millar.
The experienced exhibitor always has one eye on the judge.
Photo: Stuart.

wobbly semicircle that most novices deliver in the early days.

When you enter the ring, the steward will ask you to stand in line with the other exhibitors. The judge will call each exhibitor in turn. This is when you stand your dog to his best advantage, side-on so the judge can assess the overall balance and outline before going over your dog. The judge will put his or her hands on your Airedale and assess him in relation to the 'perfect specimen' called for in the Breed Standard. You will then be asked to walk your dog. Listen carefully to the judge's request.

Note who was the first dog to be seen, and note when all the dogs have been assessed in your class. Set your dog up and keep an eye on the judge as he or she looks along the line, deciding final positions. Placings in each class will be determined by which Airedales, in the judge's opinion, best meet the Breed Standard criteria.

All judges have preferences and so, when exhibitors enter under different judges, their placings may alter completely, or just slightly, on each occasion. Some days, your dog may not show as well; he may be overweight, underweight or lethargic, and this may affect on your placing.

EXHIBITING
We are lucky here in the UK – the Airedale Terrier as a show breed is in the hands of enthusiastic breeders. Occasionally, a handler appears in the ring, but mainly because the owner has other commitments or is unwell. Handling your dog to his best advantage is something you must practise with your Airedale. The exhibitor must allow his own conscience to guide him as to how far he can go to exhibit his dog to the best advantage within the rules.

COURTESY WHEN EXHIBITING.
One of the most important aspects when handling in the ring is never to interfere with the showing techniques of other exhibitors. Never move the dog you are handling into the rear of the dog in front. This will certainly distract the other dog and in most instances will cause him to turn and investigate. We should be polite to our neighbours on

either side, leaving adequate space, never closing the gap and stopping another dog from standing in the line; this is extremely bad manners. When you stride with your dog around the ring, do not get too close to the dog in front – leave a sensible gap.

Do not listen to those who enjoy picking faults in a winning dog. Such people specialise in 'highlighting' a fault of a certain dog, often in matters that cannot be verified without 'hands on the dog'. Gossip and backbiting is always hurtful no matter who is the object of it. The best tip is never to get involved in an injustice of this type. If you want to discuss alleged ringside travesties, do so back at home – after all, you never know who is listening at the show!

Please remember, good manners cost nothing. Always be a good sport: congratulate the winner if you lose and be gracious in victory if you win.

TIPS ON JUDGING

Quality! It's the difference between pottery and porcelain.

Andrew Brace

A common factor – the love of the breed – draws judges of all backgrounds, ages and nationalities together. Such people enter each other's lives and, as the years pass, special friendships develop. If you get hooked on showing and breeding Airedales, you may eventually be invited to become a judge of the breed. Below are some thoughts on judging that were delivered by UK judging expert Andrew Brace at a 1998 seminar for Darlington Canine Society. The talk was entitled 'Judging to the Letter'.

Why do you want to judge? What is the first thing you look for in the ring? The dog must scream its breed at you. To judge, your knowledge must be such that you can contribute something to that breed.

There is a world of difference between an all-rounder and a breed-specialist judge. Heads are important in all breeds; condition and presentation have to come into it as well, but do not get carried away. Muscle tone, which is horribly lacking in the UK, is very important and do not be fooled by flashy movement, which is such a waste of energy. Always judge as if you will never judge again and it is your last opportunity to perform as you would want posterity to judge you by.

(1) No one should contemplate judging a breed until they feel that their knowledge and understanding of that breed is such that they can contribute to its progress. Far too many people begin judging for the wrong reasons.

(2) Research and study is vital to understand a breed. Do not just look at the present-day dogs; study photographs of dogs as far back as possible and try to appreciate how breeds have developed.

(3) Breed Standards are of great importance but are virtually worthless if studied in isolation. Read your Standards in conjunction with photographs of top dogs. When a Standard describes a feature of the breed, ask yourself why it should be like that. Almost all physical requirements have their roots in the breed's original function.

(4) When appraising any dog remember that they all have faults, so spend more time ascertaining a dog's virtues than trying to seek out its shortcomings. Even the great dogs have faults – they just carry them better. Adopt a positive approach to judging. You should put dogs *up* because of their virtues, not *down* because of their faults.

(5) Remember that, as much a part of breed type as physical appearance, are temperament, carriage and bearing. When a dog walks into your ring it should scream its breed at you. Much of this is to do with demeanour.

(6) Never forget the importance of balance and outline. When you have a class lined up, imagine all those dogs painted black and try to study silhouettes. This can be very helpful, especially in marked breeds where optical illusions can play tricks.

(7) Quality is something which is very difficult to describe, but quite easy to appreciate if you have a natural 'eye'. Quality should be present in all dogs and it is a virtue which should never be underestimated, even though it is never mentioned in any Breed Standard.

(8) Heads are important in all breeds – head and expression convey individuality, personality and breed type.

(9) Movement is important, but be sure you understand what constitutes correct gait in each individual breed. What is a good movement in a Bulldog would be wholly untypical in a Poodle.

(10) When assessing movement, be sure not to neglect the profile action. 'Up and down' movement is all very well, but the action seen in profile reveals much more, since here you can see the whole animal, study its balance and proportions, its carriage and its scope. Be sure to spend time watching dogs gaiting around the ring and analyse where their legs and feet are going. Often a flashy movement which may look impressive initially is, in reality, an uneconomical action and quite untypical.

(11) When going over dogs, get into the habit of adopting the same procedure for each dog. Never start at the head with one dog, and at the tail with another: it looks so untidy and suggests a judge has no confidence, or just does not know what he is doing.

(12) When handling dogs, do so for a reason. There is no advantage in examining every square inch of a dog's surface area – especially in smooth-coated breeds – simply because it looks thorough. If you feel, feel for a reason.

(13) Watch good breed specialists at work. Not all breeds are gone over in the same manner. Certain breeds have little quirks. Lack of knowledge in this area is a real giveaway to people within the breed.

(14) Do consider condition and presentation up to a point, but never allow sophisticated grooming to blind you to a superior dog whose presentation might not be so professional. Grooming can be changed in hours. Construction and type is there for all time. Ignore people and judge dogs cold.

15 When you get a dog you really like, imagine it is owned by your worst enemy – it is still that good? Similarly, imagine a dog you do not care for being owned by your best friend – is it still that bad?

16 Make allowances for age. In some breeds, good puppies bear little resemblance to the finished adult which the Breed Standard describes. You should know what a puppy of a given age should look like in any breed. The one thing about any dog which is guaranteed to change is its age!

17 Always take note of how a dog stands after it has moved and has

Crufts – the greatest honour for a judge is to be asked to officiate at the premier dog show. This is Janet Huxley showing Ch. Robroyd Emerald at Crufts in 1992.

come to rest in a natural position. Pay more attention to this picture than the one which the handler will later create. Many dogs can be screwed into position to look quite impressive if they have a skilful handler. The dog free-standing after its gaiting is the real dog.

18 Always judge with your stomach – it is more important than your hands or your eyes. When a dog comes into the ring that gives you a gut feeling, go with it. You may make some mistakes along the way, but invariably you will be proved right in the long run.

19 When judging variety classes, remember that each dog should be judged against its own Breed Standard. Some breeds are more flashy than others, but often the 'poor relations' can produce excellent examples and they should be treated equally.

20 Always judge as if you will never judge again, and judge so that this is the appointment you will be remembered for. Far too many people make the mistake of 'bending' a little, convincing themselves that they will do it straight down the line the next time. Of course, they never do. Once you have sampled the taste of 'convenience judging' you will be lost for all time.

Andrew Brace

FINAL WORD
Food for thought for all when judging! It is your own gut feeling, courage and knowledge that will be challenged and I hope you are up to it. I enjoy judging occasionally, but deep down inside I much prefer exhibiting – being in the ring handling a new puppy. The challenge lies not only in trying to win, but in hoping the puppy will be happy and content in the ring, so that we can both socialise and interact with other puppies and their exhibitors.

9 BREEDING A LITTER

The late Mrs Jean Hopwood (a lass from the North of England) was one of the world's leading terrier authorities. At the first postwar Crufts in 1948, her Ch. Berrycroft Bedlam Bruce was Best Airedale. Jean's thoughts on breeding were "You just breed 'em, better and better each time. Don't follow the leader. You will learn by experience what dogs to use. It's all there for you if you can see. Ask questions and always listen – fools do all the talking! If you keep doing that, your breeds will benefit and this dog sport will stay alive."

BREEDING PROGRAMMES
"It's all there if you can see." Jean's words are true, exact, and to the point. How many of us do see? We may have succumbed at some stage during our breeding programmes to 'kennel blindness'. Always look scrupulously at your stock and admit to any fault or faults. The reward of breeding dogs is to produce sound, healthy specimens of the breed, and to place them in good and caring homes.

There are breeders who produce good dogs purely by planning a programme based on common sense, personal observations and years of experience. However, this experience will be gained far more slowly if it is not based on an understanding of why particular faults and virtues have been perpetuated. There are faults in every breeding line, but with careful, selective breeding they can be minimised or even eliminated, and this is good for the breed as a whole.

UNDERSTANDING GENETICS
The name genetics originates from the Greek word 'genos', meaning a race. This rapidly growing branch of biological science has possibly the most significance for us, as it deals with life itself.

Genes are hereditary factors that are passed from parent to offspring; they are the physical 'links' that are passed from one generation to the next. Each individual has thousands of genes, and they are transmitted as the entire inheritance. A string of beads is often used as the simplest way of explaining the bodies of chromosomes that carry the genes.

Chromosomes occur in pairs; the male and the female carry the same number of

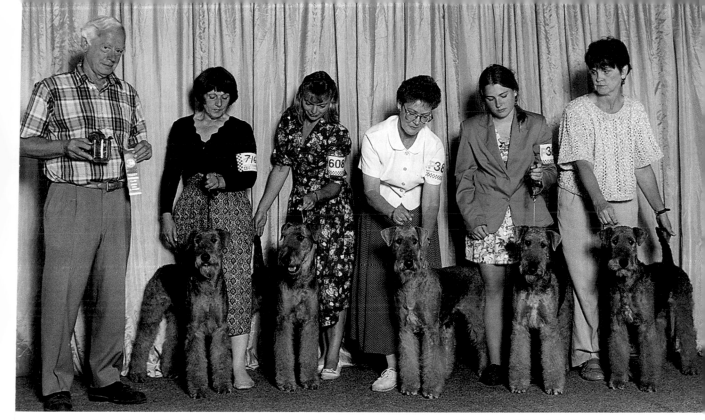

Am. Can. Ch. Huntwood's A Puppy For Dee (centre) winning Best Brood Bitch in breed at the Atlantic All-Terrier Specialty 1996. Also pictured (left to right): Ch. The Cowboy Connection, Ch. Dallas Cowboy, Ch. Cowboys Legacy and Ch. The Cowboy.

chromosomes. The offspring inherit these chromosomes, the pairs being made up of one part from the male and one part from the female. Thus inheritance comes equally from both parents. However, this may not be represented in the physical appearance or character of the individual offspring, because it depends which of the inherited factors dominate. That is why individual members of the same litter may look very different from each other, even though their parentage is the same. In essence, the science of genetics is understanding why certain characteristics are inherited in certain ways.

The vast majority of living organisms owe their existence to the union of two individuals of different sexes. To produce each new individual necessitates the combination of the minute sperm of the male with the egg of the female. The sperm and the eggs are, in effect, half-cells, and the full quota of the offspring's genes are made up as a result of cell division.

The chromosomes and genes from each parent divide, before fertilisation takes place, with one member from each pair going to form the individual offspring, and a corresponding half coming from the other parent. Therefore the contribution from each parent is a sample half of their own inheritance.

MENDELIAN GENETICS

Genes combine in many ways, and, in some pairs, one member is able to suppress the effect of its partner. This was an important genetic discovery made

correct it. The snag is that, however carefully the animal to be used as an outcross is chosen, he is almost certain to bring in not only the genes desired, but also other factors that are not wanted. Outcrossing should be regarded as an experiment, and, in a well-established strain, should not be made without good reason.

There are times when outcrossing is imperative, as when a fault or weakness occurs repeatedly in members of a certain strain, but every effort should be made to see that the animal used brings in as few alien traits, or genetic impurities, as possible. The best way to ensure this is to try and find an individual, which, though not closely related, carries some of the same foundation bloodlines as the strain with which it is to be crossed. Having made an outcross, the next step is to breed back strongly to the original line. Except in very exceptional circumstances, this is the only safe course to follow, once the purpose of outcrossing has been achieved. Only in this way can the genetic purity previously established in a valuable strain be maintained.

LINE AND FAMILY BREEDING

The close study of pedigrees is used in order to breed in and keep certain qualities. It brings into play the faith you must place in your bitch line and is one of the best methods of breeding you can use. If there are no serious faults coming to the fore, what you are doing must be correct. Nearly all the litter will be similar in type. The decision as to which puppy to keep can be really difficult. There will be more than one in the litter, which, in your eyes, is the double of a past relative.

Big Lady's kennel winning the Breeders group at the Helsinki International show, 1996. Pictured (left to right): Big Lady's Queen Regent, Int. Ch. Big Lady's Tina Turner, Big Lady's Universal Man, and Int. Ch. Big Lady's Urban Cowboy.

BREEDING REQUIREMENTS

Always remember, the bitch is the all-important anchor in your breeding programme. Without a first-rate, line-bred bitch you are wasting your time. You can use the best stud dog in the country to a third-rate bitch, and possibly get a winner from this mating, but it is unlikely to breed on.

The breeding of family (in-breeding) means parents to children, or brother to sister. It is considered a certain way to produce good stock and to set the stamp of your kennels.

Look at your pedigrees, study them and think carefully. Which will be the best method of breeding for your bitch? Look also at photographs of past members of the family; they will give you some idea of who the up-and-coming dog resembles!

Any breeding programme has to be thought out very carefully. Ask yourself the following questions. Why do I want a litter? Have I people wanting a dog or a bitch puppy? Have I enough free time to rear the litter? When will the litter be due? Have I any pressing engagements?

A bitch is not 'better' for having a litter, so do not fall into the trap of mating your bitch for this reason. Rearing a litter is costly, and takes many hours of hard work and total commitment.

THE BITCH

The bitch has to be mature and healthy. Many Airedales may not begin their first season until they are nine to 12 months of age, and some are as late as 18 months. This is normal for an Airedale. Visit the vet when your bitch is between 12 and 18 months of age and incorporate a hip-test score. It is important to have her checked over before you intend mating her, assuming she has no hereditary faults and is of good type. The X-ray of the hips must be taken well in advance of the potential mating. Avoid the procedure near to or at the onset of her season as it may affect some of the eggs. Hips can be X-rayed from twelve months of age. The average age of first mating for an Airedale bitch is two to two-and-a-half years.

THE STUD DOG

The stud dog you choose should be sound and typical of the breed in type and temperament. Think before you contemplate using a dog nearby just because he lives in your area. Look for a

Am. Ch. Bravo Star Buck: Sire of 68 Champions, he has made a huge impact on US breeding programmes.

dog that is as near the Standard as one can possibly be. He does not need to be a Champion. If you see or hear of a dog that has sired good puppies with all the characteristics of an Airedale and that also complements your bitch or possesses a particular feature that she lacks, then the choice is easy. It is also useful to ask the breeder of your bitch which stud dog they would consider best for her. It may mean travelling some distance to the dog of your choice, but this is a normal procedure used by most reputable breeders.

A fee is required for the service of the stud dog. His owner will need to know the first day of your bitch's season (bleeding from her vulva) or as near to the first day as possible, and then they will make all the necessary arrangements for your visit. You may care to leave the bitch at the stud dog's home if the owner has the facilities.

MATING
When is your bitch ready to be mated? A bitch can be ready to mate at the onset of her season and as late as her thirtieth day, but the period from the ninth to the twentieth day seems to be the norm. There are certain signs to watch for in your bitch and, here again, the stud dog owner can be a great help. While visiting the vet to have your bitch checked for any infections (most stud dog owners insist on this), you may consider having her blood-tested to ascertain the optimum day for the mating.

Mating is usually straightforward – and be aware that a 'tie' (in which the dog and bitch are linked together for what can be a considerable time) is not always necessary for conception. After the bitch is mated, the stud dog owner will usually

ask you to bring your bitch again after two days for a second mating.

The owner of the stud dog will hand you a litter registration form stating the stud dog's registered Kennel Club name, his registration number, and the date the

Eng. Am. Ch. Florac King Of Scots At Stragus: A sire of great influence, he has produced many top winners in the US, including Am. Ch. Serendipity's Eagle's Wings.

bitch was mated. They will also give you a copy of the stud dog's pedigree. You will need to keep these in a safe place. The form is for you to register the names of the resultant puppies with the Kennel Club. The pedigree is for you to write your bitch's and the stud dog's pedigrees together to form the new puppy's pedigree.

After mating, your Airedale bitch needs to be kept away from other dogs until her cycle has ended, as she may still want to mate and will still be attractive to all dogs – there could be a problem if another dog seeks and gains entry!

PREGNANCY

After the mating, assuming it has been successful, you have much to prepare. Pregnancy lasts for an average of 63 days (nine weeks) but it is normal to deliver a couple of days before or after the due date. You can have your bitch scanned by ultrasound at the appropriate stage, though this may mean travelling some distance, as such scans not widely available at veterinary surgeries. Alternatively, you may prefer leaving nature to take its course.

The bitch should stick to her normal routine; she is not sick nor an invalid, so exercise is still an important requirement. A thorough early grooming is better now than at a later stage when she will become uncomfortable with the extra weight. Food should be given as normal until you note obvious signs of pregnancy around the sixth or seventh week after mating. Signs are usually increased body weight and size of abdomen but, if the bitch is carrying only a few pups, there will be little or nothing visible. When she is lying quietly outstretched there may be some slight movement in the abdomen. This is the time to increase her normal food by around one to two thirds in quantity. Also include more protein. Do not feed her more from the onset of mating anticipating pregnancy: this may only lead to your Airedale becoming vastly overweight.

A discharge in the pregnant bitch – a sticky mucous secretion – is noticeable from the vulva usually from approximately 32 days. A bitch who shows no discharge is usually not pregnant. The quantity varies from a copious discharge hanging in strings to a mere stickiness of the hair around the vulva. The vet should be informed as to the date the bitch is due and also about any worming procedures needed before whelping. Worming will not prevent the bitch passing worms to her pups, but the best times to worm her are before mating, during pregnancy, and again when the suckling pups are old enough.

THE WHELPING QUARTERS

When you are certain your bitch is pregnant, the preparation of her quarters can begin. She must be relaxed and comfortable in the surroundings where she is to whelp. Do not leave this to the last moment, or you may find she wants to deliver on your bed! Try to maintain her feeding and sleeping in a suitable location chosen a minimum of two weeks before whelping. It should be a quiet room away from the main doors into your home. The bitch will not want visitors peeping in when she is due to deliver or when she is feeding her puppies in the early stages.

The room must be free from draughts and the temperature maintained around 25 degrees C (77 degrees F) for the first three weeks. A heat-pad or overhead heat-lamp is useful, as both of these direct warmth to a specific area. Please suspend the lamp correctly; check the required height by placing a thermometer on the floor of the box directly under the lamp and adjust accordingly. Remember also, the bitch needs to be able to walk under the lamp without it touching her!

The whelping box should be of ample size so that the bitch can lie outstretched any way she pleases, with room to spare at each end. It should have one side easily accessible for the bitch to walk in and out, but with a lip so that the puppies cannot fall out. A whelping box can be made or bought. The bedding can be of your choice, with layered newspapers for underlying insulation.

PREPARATIONS
Towards the due date, your bitch will probably be very large and less active. Her food intake will be larger and will have been divided into three or four meals a day up to the last week. Keep a close eye on her while she is out in the garden – she may dig holes and decide this is where she is going to whelp! Try to keep her brushed, tangle-free and clean. Carefully scissor the hair around her teats, underbody and vulva in readiness for the birth.

There will be more pressure on her bladder during the last two weeks and she will need to urinate more often. Lay paper down for the night just in case she cannot hold on until morning. Never scold her, as incontinence is not her fault – an Airedale bitch will herself not be happy about accidents. Remember, cuddles in the morning and a happy greeting will relax you both.

WHELPING
Items you will need are:

- A small animal feeding bottle and puppy milk (just a precaution).
- A watch.
- Pen and paper.
- Kitchen roll and lots of newspapers.
- Several old towels (kept on a warm radiator).
- Scissors.
- Sewing thread (to tie the umbilical cord if necessary).
- Baby wipes or tea-tree oil.
- A cushion for you to kneel on!

WHELPING

THE FIRST STAGE
About 24 hours (some bitches less, some more) before they are going to whelp, your bitch may refuse food. This is often quoted as an infallible signal of the onset of parturition. Most of my bitches, however, eat well up to and during the birth, so I do not find this method very useful.

Bitches scratch at the newspaper and tear at the bedding in the box and are uneasy for part of the day, followed by rest periods. The ears are pricked back and your bitch may pant. This stage can last for as long as 48 hours – so make the most of this time by preparing all the items you will need later. A baby intercom or video camera are useful so that, even when you retire to bed, you can monitor progress without disturbing the bitch too often. This allows the bitch her privacy, as it is known that sometimes a bitch may delay whelping if she feels insecure or unsafe.

During the first stage when the bitch is panting spasmodically, the cervix at the neck of the uterus is dilating (relaxing) and the pups are changing position ready for their journey. The vulva is puffy, large and very moist and begins to excrete a white or creamy discharge.

The most reliable indication of imminent whelping is a sharp drop in body temperature, which almost always occurs within 24 hours of the onset of the second stage. To pinpoint this temperature drop, you need to take the bitch's temperature over the previous week, morning and night. Remember to keep calm and relaxed when you enter the whelping area.

THE SECOND STAGE

The second stage of labour begins with a main contraction; your bitch's whole body tenses up from shoulder to rump. (Note the time in case of complications. The vet would want to know how long she has been straining.) There are intervals of rest between contractions.

If the contractions are strenuous and she is bearing down hard with no sign of delivery after one hour, seek veterinary help immediately.

The shape of the pelvis means the puppies have to climb over a hump before they can descend into the world and this takes a great deal of energy on the part of the bitch. During the latter part of the journey, the outer membrane breaks and fluid is released and exits from the vulva. This fluid is dirty and green in colour and its arrival lets you know the first pup is not far behind. A pup will usually emerge still inside the inner membrane and this may mean that you may have to help remove it. The puppy is in no danger, and the bitch may break the sac herself with her teeth, but, if she doesn't, assist her, especially if she is a maiden bitch.

Do this by breaking the sac with your fingers, allowing the bitch to help if possible. At the same time, try to keep the head of the puppy in an upright position, as this will allow fluid and mucus to flow away from the head. A quick wipe of the puppy's head with paper kitchen-roll dries the head quickly and means fluid cannot be sucked into the pup with his/her first gasp. The placenta almost always comes immediately after the whelp, and is still attached to the pup's stomach by the umbilical cord. The bitch bites this and then usually eats the placenta. If she does not, detach the cord by holding it firmly between finger and thumb of one hand and then tearing the cord with the other hand, again using finger and thumb and taking care not to pull at the stomach of the puppy. If the umbilical cord bleeds profusely, tie it off quickly using a length of sewing thread.

The placenta contains nutrients for the bitch but, in extra-large litters (more than ten), it is best not to let her eat them all. Sometimes the placenta may emerge later than the pup. Note the time of each birth and whether the placenta was also delivered.

It is quite natural for the bitch to roll her puppy and lick it after delivery; this is to dry the pup, so do not panic but let her continue. Such treatment stimulates the pup's breathing and helps to clear any fluid from the airways. The pup will usually want to suckle immediately, if the delivery was not too protracted. A long delivery can sometimes make a pup tired.

It may be that your assistance is required to encourage the pup to suckle at this stage.

Try holding the bitch's teat between forefinger and middle finger – the palm of your hand on the bitch's stomach – and hold the pup gently to the teat, working your fingers to release the milk. The puppy will usually attach itself like a leech to the teat and suckle heartily.

There is usually an interlude before the next whelp – this can be as long as four hours but as short as ten minutes. If the bitch is relaxed and not straining during contractions for a maximum of one hour, all is well, relax. Some bitches can stop whelping after six or seven puppies and still produce one or more pups the next day! Just sit and observe the wonders of nature.

Keep a bowl of fresh water available for the bitch. Also offer her milk or glucose regularly. Remember, she may, after the long hours of whelping, need to go out to relieve herself! Let the choice be hers; one can only offer her the opportunity. Food served to your bitch should be light – chicken, scrambled eggs with cheese (a favourite), cheese or fish. Provide frequent snacks, but bear in

mind that any afterbirths she has consumed may mean she has no interest in eating for a while. Her motions will naturally be slightly loose for the first few days.

When it seems that the litter is complete and the bitch is settled, change the newspapers and, if desired, carefully arrange some clean synthetic bedding. The bitch will sleep in between attending to her puppies. Monitoring the situation, at this stage, is all that should be required on your part.

Check all the puppies to make sure they have no deformities, including their mouths. Do this by placing your (clean) little finger in the mouth to check for cleft palates; the puppies should suckle. You can sex them at this stage and check the umbilical cord. A good tip is to shred newspaper lengthways in strips. The puppies cannot crawl under the paper unseen and so are always visible to the dam.

VETERINARY MATTERS

Call in the vet to visit after the bitch has finished whelping. He will check her and the pups and then give the new mother any appropriate injections. If the bitch

Ask the vet to check the puppies over when whelping is completed.

Iulius Napulotta-Grama with her puppies. Most Airedale bitches make good mothers and cope well with their puppies' demands.

looks starry-eyed, becomes restless, trembles or is not attentive to the pups, during or after delivery, call the vet straightaway and ask for a home visit. Never take your bitch to the surgery unless absolutely necessary.

BIRTH TO THREE WEEKS

It will be a busy time for you, even though the dam will be attending to the puppies. The bitch's discharge will be fairly heavy for the first few days and the process of cleansing the uterus can take as long as three to four weeks, the discharge changing from a brown colour to red and becoming lighter as the days proceed.

Some bitches will not let anyone near the pups, while others are happy to do so. A bitch I owned delivered a large litter of 12 puppies. After two days, she decided to leave seven smaller puppies in the box and carried the five larger puppies to the Vetbed provided for her outside the whelping box. I did not intervene and she fed the separated litter every hour on the hour. If your bitch decides what is to happen, leave her to it, she knows best. Do not be in a hurry to show the pups to anyone, as their dam may dislike strangers and may consequently growl or hurt a pup. Keep other animals away. Feed the bitch to

her appetite and supply light meals for the first few days.

Calcium is important for your bitch at the time, so be sure she has a good high-protein food. Feed her to appetite around four times a day. Lack of calcium brings about a condition known as eclampsia. If the level of calcium falls, she will ignore her pups, look starry-eyed, and may shake, whine or pant uncontrollably. Seek veterinary advice immediately since she could go into a coma and die. Regularly feel around the nipples to check she is not suffering from mastitis. If this happens, it can be dealt with by holding warm poultices against the hardened teat and gently squeezing out some of the milk. Always try to put one of the greedy pups on the affected teat.

Feel, do not just look at, the puppies' stomachs and make sure they are all full after suckling. If you have a pup who is not as round-bellied as the rest, encourage him as before by putting him on the teat and gently squeezing the milk to promote suckling. Sometimes, smaller puppies may be pushed out from feeding by bigger, stronger siblings. If you work hard at feed times during the first three days to make sure these puppies are fed, they will advance with the rest.

At three to four days it will be time for dewclaws and tails to be docked by a vet. This has to be arranged well in advance of the litter being born. In the UK, you need to be a member of The Council of Docked Breeds. It is not illegal to dock if the procedure is carried out by a vet.

Puppies' nails have to be kept short and this can be achieved by using scissors. The bitch will become very sore from puppies scratching and paddling as they suckle, so do attend to this.

At around ten to 15 days, the litter begin to open their eyes and but cannot see fully, as there is a film protecting the eye which restricts vision but allows reaction to light. Hearing and sight become established around the twentieth day. There is also a marked increase in the activity of the puppies

Worming needs to be carried out at around three weeks of age. Consult your vet for advice on when it is best to worm. Weighing scales must be used to calculate the bitch's weight; for the puppies you can use kitchen scales. The dosage must be accurate; never guess the pups' weight as an overdose can kill. Every puppy in the litter will be of a different weight.

WEANING

The dam will be feeling a little uncomfortable when feeding her pups around the third week, as their teeth begin to grow. She will also want to spend time away from the pups but not out of earshot. The solution is to provide her with a separate bed area so that the pups cannot reach her, and she can lie comfortably without being pestered. Now is the time to begin weaning, encouraging the litter to lap a milky porridge specially developed for puppies. This is a messy time for all, but what fun to watch! The bitch, at this stage, will be eating an unbelievable amount of food. I have known a bitch to consume as much as four to six times her normal amount of food.

It may also be time to move the puppies and mum into different quarters if you have not already done so, as there is a need for more space at this stage.

Weaning usually starts at around three weeks – and it does not take the puppies long to get the idea! Photo: Amanda Bulbeck.

The puppies begin to climb out of the box to play and relieve themselves. Airedales are clean by nature and most will not soil their sleeping area. The bitch may not want to clean up after the puppies any longer. This is the time when all the old newspapers will be used to the fullest extent. Put many layers of papers on the floor of the puppy area; when soiled they can be easily rolled up and disposed of. Rubber gloves are useful, as are some disinfectants (check they are safe for puppies), a mop and plastic sacks to dispose of the paper.

There are many foods on the market and complete foods do make life easier when weaning. Feed every three hours in the beginning, and gradually decrease to every four hours (five feeds a day). Always make the last feed of the day about an hour before you retire to bed. If the puppies eat it all quickly, you may not have served sufficient amounts. Remember the slow eaters in the litter. Take the food away after an hour in case of flies. Let Mum back in after feeding time, as she will always finish the leftovers. Feed puppies to appetite and have fresh water down at all times.

Even when the puppies are fully weaned, their mother will still want to feed them occasionally and she may, around the six-week stage, bring up partially digested food for them. A few words on diet: cooked eggs are fine, but

112

never feed raw egg-white to any dog since it is almost indigestible. Complete foods and canned meats cater for every age and stage of dog. Cod-liver oil and vitamins should only be given if the diet is poor, as they may upset the digestive system.

SOCIALISING PUPPIES

Puppies need to become accustomed to being handled at around four weeks of age and must receive plenty of attention if they are to become well-adjusted pets.

From eight weeks, if they bite you, growl at them just as their mother does if they require it. Provide toys for them to chew. Give lots of free play with mum in the garden where they can explore, exercise and become fit. When you call the litter's mother, her puppies will usually follow and this is another learning process in their life. Clatter their bowls at mealtimes and place a radio in their quarters; different sounds and surroundings make for bold well-adjusted puppies ready for their new owners.

SELLING THE PUPPIES

When interested parties visit the litter as prospective buyers, do vet them carefully. Pry a little into their background. It will reassure you to know that each puppy is going to a caring home. Selling the litter usually happens at the age of eight weeks.

Have everything prepared when the new owners arrive for their puppy. Is the pedigree at hand and the registration ready to sign over at the time of sale? Compile a guide to the puppy's routine, feed times and when worming is due again. It is worth mentioning puppy insurance, provided by many animal insurance companies. The puppy would

thus be insured for the first six or eight weeks after leaving you, depending on the policy. After payment, the puppy leaves for his new home and legally your responsibility ends.

However, responsibility does not end there for the caring breeder, even though you hope you have found the perfect family. If by chance the new owners have some crisis and the dog has to be re-homed, I would hope they can seek your help by bringing the puppy or dog back to you for re-homing or that you can give caring assistance by putting them in touch with Airedale Rescue. This situation can and does happen occasionally and rescue societies may have a client waiting for an older dog, rather than a puppy.

The responsible breeder takes a huge amount of care when the time comes to sell the puppies. Photo: Amanda Bulbeck.

10 *AIREDALES IN THE UK*

AMBASSADORS OF THE BREED
The ambassadors of our breed do not just meander in. Behind these Airedales are breeding programmes which we, as breeders, will never forget.

One of the greatest of winners was Ch. Riverina Tweedsbairn (Ricky) He was Supreme Best in Show Crufts 1961, handled by Joe Cartledge and owned by Miss Pat McCaughey and Mrs D. (Mac) Schuth (Riverina Kennels). Ricky was also Top Dog All Breeds in 1960 and 1961.

Mary Swash was the person behind the scenes at Crufts in 1961, Ricky being her dog, as she did everything for him. Mary did not take him into the ring on that great occasion, but she had shown him to some of his great wins at other shows. The South of England Airedale Terrier Club holds a Tweedsbairn party in his honour every year the weekend after Crufts.

Ch. Perrancourt Playful was born on February 9th 1977 (Am. Ch. Turith Adonis x Perrancourt Preview), bred by Paul and Dot Hanks. For the first ten months of her show career she was handled by Dot. In May 1978, she was handled by the 'King', Ernest Sharpe.

Her first CC was at Leeds in June 1978, her second with BoB at Three Counties, and her title was gained at Blackpool just three weeks later. From then on she won the bitch CC at every show in which she was entered. She won, in all, 35 CCs and was the Breed record holder (until recently), winning BoB on 29 occasions, including Crufts 1979 and 1980 and three breed club shows in 1979. Her list of credits: 13 terrier groups at General Championship Shows, BIS at the National Terrier Club, Reserve BIS at WELKS (West of England Ladies' Kennel Show), Birmingham City, Scottish Kennel Club, and Belfast; Best in Show at Bath and Blackpool. She was third in the Champions of Champions contest and was Top Champion Bitch. Her show successes in 1979 made her Top Dog All Breeds. Playful was without doubt an outstanding Champion, admired by all. Many stated she was the finest Airedale ever seen. Paul Hanks speaks of 'Maddy' thus: "Apart from her successful show career she endeared herself at home to everyone she met with her charming

Ch. Ginger Xmas Carol: Crufts Supreme Best in Show 1986.

(although somewhat wily character) and was truly a great ambassador for the breed."

The acclaimed Ginger kennels in Italy (Dginger in the UK) are owned by Alessandra Sommi Picenardi (known affectionately as Cucca). Ch. Ginger Xmas Carol (Emma), was born in Italy on Christmas Day in 1982 and bred from two English Airedales, Int. Ch. Drakehall Diadem and Int. & Eng. Ch. Double Dutch of Clare. Emma's early guidance and training came from Annette Hall who was staying with Cucca at the time. Annette is a Yorkshire lass who enjoys working her dogs, so Emma was taught all the rudiments of retrieving and obeying commands. Emma came to the UK and stayed in quarantine at Liz Cartledge's kennels, Ryslip. She then went to live at the Jokyl kennels and was prepared and handled always by Mary Swash. Emma was Supreme Best in Show at Crufts 1986 and is the second Airedale ever to win this award. To add to her fantastic awards, she was Top Airedale, Top Terrier and second Best Dog All Breeds 1985, as well as Top Brood bitch 1990. Adding to her list of honours were five

Ch. Balintober Envoy For Jokyl: Pup of the Year All Breeds 1992, Top Airedale 1993.

Best in Show awards, 15 Terrier group wins at General Championship shows, and four BIS at breed club Championship Shows. Emma died, aged 12, in Italy in June 1995.

Mary Swash speaks of Ricky and Emma as absolutely wonderful show dogs with personalities that made them easy to show. Both could bring out something extra when it counted, and rose to the big occasions.

Repeatedly producing typical, healthy, sound generations of Airedales proves that Jokyl partners, Mary Swash and Olive Jackson, have an eye for "a good 'un". Mary has had a great deal of experience with top winning dogs. Ch. Jokyl Gallipants (Soldier) was Top Dog All Breeds 1983, Top Airedale 1984, Top Airedale Sire 1985, Top Stud dog

1985/6/7 and 1990-95. He was also Top Terrier Stud Dog 1986 and 1992. The proud father of 25 English Champions, he has won all the major competitions except Crufts. His final appearance in the show ring was in 1995 at Crufts, retiring in true glory having won BoB. Soldier was Mary's ideal in a dog, as well as a great showman. Gallipants's sire is Ch. Siccawei Galliard, another top dog and sire of 17 English Champions.

The top winner in the breed today is living with her handler and co-breeder Mary Swash at the Jokyl kennels. Ch. Jokyl This Is My Song, known as Nan (Ch. Jokyl Gallipants x Ch. Ginger Dancing Song), was owned by Gladys Coxall but is now owned by her breeders. She began her show career in 1992 winning Best Puppy in Show at the National Terrier. Her first CC was in October at the Midland Counties ATC the same year. Her title came in October 1993, making a total of four CCs that year. In 1994 she won 17 CCs, in 1995 she took 14, and she was Top Terrier 1996, gaining five CCs.

At the National Airedale Championship Show in April 1999, judged by Mr A. Favell (Alshadlie), Nan took yet another CC with BoB from veteran class, and again at Southern Counties, judged by Stig Ahlberg (Ragtime). Also at Windsor in July 1999 she took BoB under Debbie Graham (Stanstead) with Terrier Group 2, proving that at eight years of age she can still stand with the best and beat them.

Nan is on record for winning the most CCs in the breed, probably for all time. To date she has 45 CCs to her credit, winning RBIS Crufts 1996, Top Airedale 1994, 1995 and 1996, and 13 Championship Show Groups.

Ch. Ballintober Gold Of Saredon (Saredon The Jazzsinger x Junaken Valetta), bred by Bernie Frost and owned by Judy Averis, had a marvellous career in the UK. He won 16 CCs, two Groups and Reserve BIS, and was Top Airedale 1990. He then went to Germany to the home of Mrs Weckmüller-Führer in Kassel and was handled by Jack Houben. 'Gold' acquired many a Championship title: UK, Netherlands, Luxembourg (1991-3), World (1991-2), International, French, Klub Champion (Germany, Holland, Austria, Belgium), Eurodog and Austrian Bundessieger. In total he gained 32 CCs.

Ch. Ballintober Envoy For Jokyl was bred by Bernie Frost and owned by Mary Swash and Olive Jackson. He had a fantastic show career at a tender age and was Winalot/Dog World Pup of the Year 1992 as well as Top Airedale 1993.

Ch. Cocas Cosmos (Cocas Cola x Cocas Topsy Turvy) was taken to his English title at the age of 15 months by his owner/breeder Jean Rendall (Cocas). He left our shores and went to live with his new owner Helga Fleischer (vom Tannenbruch). Jack Houben handled Cocas throughout his fantastic showing career. He won many Championships – English, Danish, Dutch, Luxembourg, World, French, International, Winner Amsterdam, Klub Champion Dutch, Belgium, Swiss, French, German and Eurodog. During his show career his wins totalled 59 CCs, 13 Res CCs, 21 BoBs and four BIS.

Ch. Robroyd Granite (breeder/owner Tom and Janet Huxley) is, to date, the only Airedale to have achieved the honour of winning three CCs with two BoB in puppy classes. Granite gained his crown, with his fourth CC with BoB, only just out of puppy, from the junior class at Leeds in July 1993. This made the double for this kennel, with Robroyd Emerald Pride at Tiggis winning the

Ch. Robroyd Granite: The only Airedale to win three CCs with two BoBs from the puppy class.

Bitch CC. Granite's sire Diamond won the CC and Emerald CC with BoB, making another double for this small kennel. During his short showing career, Granite won in the breed, six Best Puppy, five CCs, four BoB, three Reserve CCs, one BIS and three Reserve BIS, and was Top Puppy 1993 (and runner-up Top Dog the same year), as well as Top Sire 1995 and 1998, and Top Stud in 1997.

Ch. Saredon Handyman was Top Airedale 1987 and 1988. He is also on record as the Top Winning Airedale Male with 33 CCs to his credit.

Ch. Saredon The Jazzsinger was Top Airedale 1986.He ended his brilliant show career by winning the veteran class with BoB at Crufts in 1991, at the age of seven-and-a-half. This made a total of 25 CCs.

TODAY'S LEADING KENNELS

Who will be the UK's next Airedale Supreme Champion? Even great dogs need a bit of luck and a good combination of judges, together with handling and presenting the dog to his best advantage.

However, the show scene starts and ends with breeding good dogs. The rest is icing on the cake. The following kennels are currently breeding some of the best Airedales to be found in this country.

ALSHADLIE – Al Favell (formerly Shadli – Al and Jan Favell)
The kennel's first Champion in 1981 was a bitch, Ch. Shadli Adorn (Wellington of Lionsdown of Searchlight x Shadli Partypiece), a real showgirl with super temperament. The famous Searchlight

kennel of Millie Kington, who is now in her nineties, provided the basis for Shadli, with Siccawei and Bengal for the male line. Two bitches were bought in: from the late Les Atkinson (Judy Averis's father) came Turith Baroness (Ch. Siccawei Galliard x Prelude of Turith) and from Pat Crome came Tintara Arctus (Ch. Siccawei Galliard x Tintara Persephone). These bitches carried the same bloodlines, so Shadli's programme was set. Since then, in 1974, every litter bred has produced Championship winning stock.

In 1984, Shadli bred and showed the top winning Airedale bitch in Britain with nine CCs, three BoBs and a Reserve CC. This was Ch. Shadli Classy Charmer (Ch. Siccawei Galliard x Shadli Partypiece), who also produced Ch. Shadli Fantom (sire of Ch. Jokyl Gallipants). Another star was Ch. Shadli Likely Lad or 'Matt' (Ginger Voila of Stanstead x Shadli Bellona). In his first eight shows, he took eight Firsts, four Best Puppy in Breed and a Reserve CC, and gained his junior warrant, puppy stakes class, against 400 entries at Darlington Championship Show where he was placed third. He also won the Pedigree Chum/Top Puppy award. Later in his career, at the LKA (Ladies, Kennel Association) Championship Show, he took BoB and went on to be placed third in the Terrier Group. He and his brother, Shadli Lord Luke, went on to become International Champions, as did many others from this kennel.

BALLINTOBER – Bernie Frost
A quiet but strong influence in the heart of Scotland is Ballintober breeder Bernie Frost. Ch. Ballintober Envoy For Jokyl was Pup of the Year All Breeds 1992

(Ch. Jokyl Gallipants x Ballintober Coco). 'Toby' won 16 CCs, two Groups and a RBIS. He was owned by Olive Jackson and Mary Swash and was Top Airedale 1993. His dam, Ballintober Coco, was Top Brood Bitch 1994.

Ch. Ballintober Gold Of Saredon, Top Airedale 1990, is another of Bernie's dogs that has produced many quality Champions here and abroad. In the UK he sired Ch. Junken Vision, Ch. Saredon Start The Fire, Ch. Robroyd Emerald, Ch. Robroyd Emerald Pride At Tiggis and Ch. Codale Touch Of Gold.

Ch. Ballintober An Teallack (Jokyl Gallipants x Ballintober Coco) was made a Champion in 1994. Another of Bernie's dogs gaining Top Puppy in 1997 was Ballintober Tor Of Robroyd (Ch. Robroyd Granite x Ballintober Chloe).

Bernie says of her approach to line-breeding: "Try not to introduce too many different lines or you will fail to produce your type."

BEACYTAN – Berit Forsman
Berit's first Airedale was bought in 1977, a Bengal dog who never seemed to stop growing as a pup, reaching an impressive 27 inches to the shoulder when mature. He failed to get any placing at any show ever, but was a great dog, a good companion, kind and considerate, and he is the reason Berit became hooked on the breed.

The kennel's foundation bitch came from the Loudwell line. In her first litter she produced Beacytan Alikhazam, Berit's first successful show dog. In the same litter were two sisters, Beacytan Alison and Beacytan Alibi, who became very important in the future breeding programme. Alison was a big bitch, with

Ch. Beacytan Troubadour: Sired by Ch. Am. Ch. Blackjack's Nostradamus.

the stamp of a good potential brood bitch (well-proportioned and not exaggerated in any way) and she produced the kennel's first Champion, Beacytan Gay Paree. In the same litter, there was also a male, Beacytan Gay Fawks, who sired the second, Ch. Beacytan Koh-I-Noor.

Alibi produced Beacytan Be A Princess, a Champion in Sweden, and a litter sister, Beacytan Be A Honey, who won a lot in the show ring in England and, in time, whelped Berit's seventh Champion, Beacytan Vanilla.

Am. Ch. Blackjack's Nostradamus was imported from the US, and he was to become a very important addition to the Beacytan gene bank. Nostradamus brought with him excellent temperament, rich colours and good

Ch. Beacytan Clairvoyant.

movement. He was also very short-coupled and tall, which made him look very impressive. He passed many of these qualities on to his progeny.

Gay Paree and Nostradamus produced the first homebred male Champion – Ch. Beacytan Troubadour, who turned out to be the spitting image of his dad with a bit of mother thrown in.

Koh-I-Noor and Nostradamus came up with Finnish and Int. Ch. Beacytan Xerxes, and brother Ch. Beacytan Xavier in Sweden.

Another excellent brood bitch, Beacytan Fantasia, really clicked with Nostradamus. In her first litter she had 15 puppies all of whom survived and from whom Berit had two English Champions, Ch. Beacytan Serendipity and Ch. Beacytan Silver Dollar, plus Int. Ch. Beacytan Stars And Stripes. Their litter sister, Beacytan Silver Screen, was very lightly shown, but became a proud mum to the ninth Champion, Ch. Beacytan Clairvoyant.

In 1990, Berit imported another male from the US, Britham Out And About, in order to broaden the gene pool. His bloodline was very interesting, going back to big names over there, which nicely complemented the input from Nostradamus.

Out And About was an excellent mover, a quality that he has passed on to his children. He also had an excellent head. He produced with Vanilla a good litter, containing Beacytan Nemesis, Champion in France, and Beacytan Nerone who, in turn, is the sire of several interesting litters.

Berit considers a strong bitch line to be very important and counts Prelude Of Turith as one of the most impressive broods. Prelude did not win much in the show ring but produced quality puppies with every male she was mated to. She is the great-grand dam of Beacytan's 'S' litter, and is also featured in the pedigree of Britham Out And About.

Another impressive brood bitch, who was also a great show dog, was Jokyl Smartie Pants.

Among the males, Berit's favourite dog is Am. Eng. Ch. Blackjack's Nostradamus. He was also Top Sire for two years running 1988-89, producing eight English Champions in the short time he stayed in England. He moved to Sweden after two years to live with Berit's niece and co-owner.

GLENTOPS – Keith McCallum
Beryl McCallum fell in love with the Airedale Terrier as a child and later founded her Glentops kennel in the mid-1960s after acquiring a daughter of Searchlight Pinswell Xchequer out of Bess Beloved, which she named Jenny Of Glencorrie. A second bitch,

Glencorrie Coquette, a daughter of Ch. Searchlight Tycoon out of Suliston Flayre, was next to join the kennel and both bitches were mated to Searchlight stud dogs to establish a line under the Glentops affix.

Following several years of 'apprenticeship' in the breed, this small select kennel became active on the Championship Show circuit and, in 1981, produced its first Champion, Ch. Glentops Krackerjack (Ch. Turith Brigand x Glentops Eloquence). Krackerjack was all showman in the ring, standing foursquare with that air of superiority, and the conformation of an outstanding specimen to back it up. His legs were ramrods of solid bone, the topline firm as a rock, the overall impression was one of power, a small dark eye set right gave true expression, and his coat and colour left nothing to be desired.

When moving, he was one of the best, free-flowing with plenty of drive from the rear; there was an athletic precision about it so rarely seen today. An Airedale of class from stem to stern, one of the nicest things about him was a penchant for mischief with a totally happy disposition. This he displayed throughout his short life, during which he won 14 CCs, the Terrier Group at Blackpool Championship Show and the Terrier Group and BIS at the Paignton All Breeds Championship Show in 1981.

The late George Leatt, after awarding him BoB said: "Ch. Glentops Krackerjack was bang on, looking the part and moving stylishly, he lives up to his name and it is worthy of mention that we had many of his progeny at this show. He has proved that he is worthy to be in the stud book and could prove a real pillar in the breed."

Sadly, this was not to be, for Krackerjack died at five years of age, the victim of a bee sting just as his stud potential was about to be realised.

His son, Gay Charlie of Glentops became an Int., German and Swiss Champion, twice World Champion in 1981 and 1983, European Champion in 1983, and won Club Seiger in 1983.

Three of his daughters became British Champions. The first Ch. Glentops Ocean Breeze out of Glentops I'm A Lady, took her title in 1981. A fiery madam, quite fearless, she was always ready to assert her dominance over other dogs and, because of this old-fashioned terrier trait, could be difficult to handle. Her biggest day came when she topped the bill, defeating Krackerjack, the dog CC winner, for BIS at the National Airedale Championship show of that year, under breed judge Ray Keith.

Breeze was a short-backed, compactly made bitch with a superb hard coat and colour, good reach of neck giving a super top line, and she had a well-balanced head piece and sound movement. Breeze took everyone's heart with her forceful character and was well known for her terrier gameness.

Another Krackerjack daughter, a sister to Ocean Breeze, was Ch. Glentops Ocean Mist who took her title in 1983. Mist was a calmer version of her firecracker sister, true to type, balanced with a short firm back, superb movement with power and drive which demonstrated her soundness and lovely outline in the show ring.

The following year saw the last of Krackerjack's progeny to take her Champion title when, in 1984, Ch. Glentops Raggity Ann won this accolade. 'Gypsy', as she was known at home, was a lovable bundle of pure mischief whose dam was the aptly named Danish Ch. Glentops Mischief Maker. Combining elegance of outline with an overall impression of the breed's lasting toughness and endurance, Gypsy possessed one of the richest of tan coats, its texture as hard as bristle, and complemented by a jet-black saddle. She was a cracker.

In 1988, Ch. Glentops Trick Or Treat, a great-grandson of Krackerjack, emerged out of a mating between Ch. Saredon The Jazzsinger and Glentops Yorkshire Rose. He won his title early in the year with CCs at Manchester, National Terrier Club and the West of England and LKA Championship Shows. Rusty was, and is at the time of writing, the epitome of an Airedale gentleman, laid back and prepared to get along with anything on two or four legs. In the ring he was alert, up on his toes and usually wagging his tail in greeting. All of his six CC wins were under breed or terrier experts who appreciated his classical conformation.

Over the years Glentops stock has gained Champion titles in Denmark, Germany, Switzerland, Finland, USA and South Africa, while Beryl is an international judge of the breed having judged as far afield as the Argentine and South Africa.

SUJONCLA – Sue Seabridge
When Sue bought her first Airedale, she had spent a number of years in her youth showing and breeding Great Danes and Poodles. She also spent time showing and breeding horses. Later, she became more involved in the working aspect of animals, so branched out into the Working Trials with Spaniels.

Her interest in terriers led Sue and husband John into Airedales. Sue's main concern was to acquire an Airedale that could do the job of work that he was bred for. The two kennels that really interested her were Glentops and Saredon, for their unrivalled movement, working ability and temperament.

Sujoncla's foundation bitch, Glentops Aimin' High (1984-96) was out of Ch. Glentops Raggity Ann x Ch. The Deerhunter Of Saredon. This bitch was everything that Sue wanted in an Airedale; she was the kennel's basis then and will continue to be so.

JOKYL – Mary Swash
Mary Swash is partner in the Jokyl kennels and has bred and owned or handled many Champions. Her secret of success as a breeder/exhibitor is to keep her very best animals. Her advice is to have faith in the chosen ones and keep them through all the ugly and ungainly stages (which, with Airedales, can last quite a while!), and breed the dog to the best in the breed that appears suitable – in the case of a male allow other breeders to use him and try to buy the best you can from the best bitch he has mated.

When asked to select a typical Jokyl Airedale from long list of memorable dogs, Mary chose 'Cedric', because of his great character. Cedric or Jokyl Smart Set, never did manage to win his third CC; when other dogs in the Open class were having a good old go at each other Cedric would steadfastly turn his back on it all. He was only really on his toes when there was a bitch around. Everyone who came to Jokyl knew and loved Cedric. He had a birthday party every year and even received his own birthday and Christmas cards; in fact he had a real fan club.

JUNAKEN – Ken Ventress
As a teenager, Ken started showing Wire-Haired Fox Terriers along with his father. He then bought an Airedale pup and had some good wins with her, which inspired him to buy another. A few BIS followed, which led Ken on to breeding, and, from the litter, he kept a dog and a bitch. The dog, Junaken Vagabond gained two CCs. The rest of the litter went to various parts of the country, but more went abroad, where some gained their titles.

Ken and his wife June approached Ernest Sharpe, who had two six-month-old bitches for sale. One was brave and

the other frightened, but Ken chose the nervous one. She was called Debby. The couple worked hard with this bitch, socialising and spending lots of quality time with her. After three months, on her first outing, Drakehall Debra of Junaken went BIS.

At one show Mary Swash was showing a young dog, Jokyl Gallipants, for the first time. Ken thought he was so outstanding he decided there and then to use this dog on Debby, as his breeding suited hers. Ken is a firm believer in line-breeding, finding that it keeps faults to a minimum.

From three litters, Debby produced a total of 12 Champions at home and abroad. She died at the age of 12 leaving an outstanding bitch line.

Junaken can boast Champions in New Zealand, Norway, Sweden, Germany, Japan, America, Brazil and Argentina.

KARUDON – Ruth Millar
Ruth is owner/breeder of the Karudon kennels and an ardent exhibitor for well over 20 years. Ch. Karudon Kalypso (Jokyl Smart Set x Karudon Kastor Sugar) was her Crufts bitch CC winner in 1984 and Reserve Top Airedale bitch for the same year, winning seven CCs, two BoB, BIS and four reserve CCs.

Over the past ten years, her winning dogs (not necessarily Champions) were Ch. Karudon Kuddle Up, Ch. Karudon Klose Kontact, Ch. Karudon Karlah, Ch. Flojo Forget Me Not At Karudon, Karudon Kavalry Man and Karudon Koronilla.

Ch. Karudon Kalypso produced two UK Champions, three overseas Champions, several with one or two CCs and many with reserve CCs. Karudon Kosie Days produced one UK

Ch. Junaken Vision: Group and BIS winner.

Ch. Karudon Kalypso: Crufts CC winner.

Champion, and Ch. Karudon Klose Kontact sired one UK Champion.

Ruth has kept to the same bitch line for over 20 years, as many good breeders do. She rarely keeps a male, preferring to use dogs of similar type and bloodline to her bitches. To crown 1999, Ruth's bitch Ch. Karudon Koronilla became Top Airedale bitch, winning six CCs. She is a lovely, compact bitch with free-flowing movement. Her sire is Ch. Jokyl Ambassador and her dam is Flojo Forget Me Not At Karudon.

Ruth is also much admired as a Championship Show judge and has judged in many countries outside the UK. During 1999, she judged Airedale Terriers at Crufts and in Moscow.

MATRASEN – Stephanie and Mark Holbrook
After several years absence from the show ring, this kennel recently enjoyed showing the dog Saredon The Terminator For Matrasen who gained his junior warrant and three reserve CCs. The Holbrooks then obtained from Judith Averis a five-year-old Gallipants daughter, Saredon Mystery Girl, whose mother, Saredon Uptown Girl, was a full sister to Saredon The Jazzsinger. She was bred to Ch. Saredon Handyman and they retained two puppies: a dog, Matrasen Galloping Gourmet (who retired early due to a road accident at the age of just 17 months, after winning his junior warrant and two reserve CCs) and a bitch puppy, Matrasen Gentle Smackaroo, who won her first CC then retired to have a litter by Ch. Robroyd Granite.

The retained bitch puppy, Matrasen Canterbury Belle (one reserve CC), was mated to a Matrasen Galloping Gourmet son, Ch. Matrasen Smart Alec J.W.

A bitch puppy was purchased by Voiko and Toja Zidar and exported to Slovenia. In early 1999, she became Int. Ch. Matrasen On Cue For Sapienti, having previously been second Top Airedale in Italy 1998. The same year also saw the rise of Matrasen Smart Alec J.W. to his Champion title, gaining six CCs and three reserve CCs. A litter brother, handled by his owner, Joseph Ocenasek, became Czech & Polish Ch. Matrasen Swingtime. A lightly-shown full brother to these two, Matrasen Assassin, won his first reserve CC, and two of his littermates, Matrasen Avenger and Matrasen Amore, picked up a Green Star and reserve Green Star on the Irish circuit. The mother of these two litters

Ch. Matrasen Smart Alec JW. Winner of six CCs.

was Florac Whiskey Jean (line-bred to Stargus Sea King).

The Holbrooks are currently showing Matrasen Flash That Cash and Matrasen Fantasia, who are sired by Ch. Saredon Light My Fire out of Matrasen Gentle Smackaroo.

ROBROYD – Tom Huxley
A nearby litter for sale, of Mynair and Saredon breeding, in November 1984, provided the Huxleys with Gem, "a special girl", from whom all of their lines are descended. Rob-Royd Gem was the name they chose; having no affix at the time. Her lineage traces back to Siccawei, Bengal and Kresent. On the dam's side was complete Mynair breeding, including Gem's great-great-great-grand-dam, Ch. Iona of Mynair. Gem's sire was Ch. The Deerhunter Of Saredon, in whose sire's background is

the dam Prelude Of Turith (Judy Averis' third foundation bitch). Prelude's great-grandsire was Ch. Optimist Of Mynair.

In 1986, the Huxleys acquired a puppy, Ch. Shadli Magnum of Robroyd (Ch. Jokyl Gallipants x Shadli Bellona), from the Shadli 'M' litter. Magnum was a faithful housedog and their first show Champion, placed second in the Terrier Group at Driffield Championship Show under the well-known terrier specialist Joan Langstaff.

Gem, mated to the Shadli dog Eng. Ch. Likely Lad, produced the couple's very first 'Gems' in 1987, and two bitches, Brazilianite and Bronzite, were kept. Bronzite was the bitch CC winner for Wilma Carter (USA) when she judged our NATC Breed Championship Show. Bronzite excelled as a showgirl and was the dam of Robroyd Champions Flint and Granite.

Eng. Ital. Ch. Robroyd Jet: Top Airedale in Italy 1996 and 1997.

Magnum and Gem produced lovely Airedales for their novice breeders. Crystal, a bitch from the second litter, took her CC under Terrier specialist Barbara Jull. Crystal was Top Brood Bitch 1992.

Magnum and Brazilianite produced the 'D' litter. Robroyd Diamond (Top Sire 1993) never enjoyed the ring, taking one CC and two reserve CCs. His litter sister Black Diamond won two CCs and three reserve CCs.

Crystal produced the fourth or 'E' litter of 12 puppies. The Huxleys kept two bitches, one of whom was Ch. Robroyd Emerald (sire Ch. Ballintober Gold at Saredon). Emerald was Crufts bitch CC winner from junior class, and collected six CCs, four reserve CCs, three BoB, Terrier Group 2, and Top Airedale Bitch 1992. German judge Rudi Tegeler said in his critique of Emerald: "The bitch has but one fault – she is not in my kennels." Her litter sister Ch. Robroyd Emerald Pride at Tiggis was at the time owned by Peter Dugdill (Tiggis).

Flint was exported after winning one CC with BoB at the National Terrier Show and three reserve CCs. Now Ital. and Int. Ch. Robroyd Flint (Ch. Shadli Magnum Of Robroyd x Robroyd Bronzite), Flint was Italy's Top Dog and Club Champion in1994, winner of the Terrier Group (Harry O' Donohue), two Group 2s and a Group 4 for owners Marco and Alex Galli (Lisander).

Aunt and nephew produced the next litter which gave the Huxleys Ch. Robroyd Granite (Robroyd Diamond x Robroyd Bronzite). Both lines from the 'B' litter were brought together (Diamonds' dam being Brazilianite, Bronzite's sister), for the kennel's sixth generation. Granite was Top Puppy 1993 and runner-up Top Airedale Dog that year, Top Sire 1995, Top Stud 1997 and Top Sire 1998.

Granite is the only Airedale to win three CCs while still in puppy classes. He was a Champion with his fourth CC at just over twelve months of age. In Tom Huxley's opinion, Granite has all the best of sound attributes any dog can possess.

Emerald Pride came back home to stay after gaining her Champion status with her owner Peter Dugdill (Tiggis) and, in her first litter ('J'), she produced two Champions sired by Granite. Ch. Robroyd Jewel gained seven CCs, ten reserve CCs, two BIS and reserve BIS at the Airedale Championship Show and a Group 4 at Leeds, and was Top Winning Bitch 1996 (having gained the most CCs that year). Her litter brother, Eng. Ital. Int. Ch. Robroyd Jet, won two of his CCs in puppy class towards his title of English Champion. Jet was Top Airedale in Italy 1996 and 97, and Sieger Winner and S.I.T. (Sociale Italia Terriers) 1997, and is also owned by the Gallis.

Emerald then produced her only litter of three bitches sired by Granite, two of whom, Lazurite and Lignum, both have one CC with BoB, and two and three reserve CCs respectively. The third bitch from Emerald's litter, Lapis Lazuli, is enjoying Obedience work and charity displays.

Opal (R. Granite x R. Emerald Pride), another quality bitch, went to Enrico Nicolini and Antonella Girgi in Como, Italy and is now an Italian Champion.

Before Jet left for Italy, he sired Robroyd Ruby, whose dam was Robroyd Imperial Jade (R. Granite x R.

Ch. Robroyd Jewel: Top-winning bitch, 1996. Photo: John Hartley.

Black Diamond). Ruby took the National Airedale Terrier Championship Show by storm at just six months old, winning minor puppy under judge Leslie Lee (Stargus). Jewel, her aunt, also took BIS that day. Ruby has produced, from a mating with grandsire Granite, the 'T' litter, a dog, Robroyd Titaneum (two reserve CCs to date), and a bitch, Robroyd Topaz.

RUSTAM – Janet Callon
Janet has been in Airedales all her life, her grandfather, William Henry Steele, being one of the early breeders from Bingley. Her first Airedale bitch, bought in 1970, was of pure Burdale lines and was mated to Ch. Lukenias Trawlerman Of Burdale. This litter produced the first Rustam show bitch, Rustam Little Model, who obtained two reserve CCs. This bitch was mated to Ch. Tamworth Merriment and produced Rustam Christmas Rose, who won a CC at the age of 18 months. Hopes of a great show career were dashed when she escaped and returned with a badly broken leg. Her grand-daughter was mated to Ch. Robroyd Granite, producing the kennel's latest show bitch, Rustam Lady In Red (one CC and six reserve CCs) to date.

SAREDON – Judy Averis and David Scawthorne
Judy's father (Les Atkinson) was a stickler for movement in dogs, and his daughter wanted a line that produced good colour, black with a rich tan, which really stands out in the ring, plus a harsh coat to work on.

Judy liked Clare Halford's Siccawei breeding, so she purchased two bitch puppies out of a litter from Ch. Siccawei

Kings Ransom x Siccawei Q.E.Too, in order to start her own line under the Saredon affix.

The bitch that Judy showed became Ch. Cilleine Penelope; the other, named Picturesque Of Saredon, was not such a good showgirl. Bred to Ch. Bengal Flamboyant, she produced group winner Ch. Bengal Saladin, sold to Mollie Harmsworth. A Bengal dog was used because in the Siccawei lines Clare had regularly used Bengals.

When Penelope ended her show career a suitable mate was found at the Jokyl kennels, Ch. Siccawei Galliard. He produced many beautiful puppies, including two males, Saredon Sir Duke and Saredon Military Man. Duke was a wonderful dog but never became a Champion, while Military Man won a CC and was sold to America where he soon gained his title and produced many top Champions.

Judy's next purchase was another bitch puppy named Prelude Of Turith who had all the makings of a Top brood, if not a showgirl. She went to live with Beryl Blower of Turith Airedales as a house pet and brood. Prelude was out of a Siccawei dam, Siccawei African Violet, and Galliard was selected as sire.

Prelude became an Airedale legend and from her first two litters produced Am. Ch. Turith Adonis and Ch. Turith Brigand, and also Turith Barbaro for Beryl, who campaigned him to one CC. He then became a top sire in Europe.

A beautiful dog, who won two CCs in England before being sold to America, Adonis was the only Airedale Terrier to win the coveted Rose Bowl eight times. He was also the Top Sire All Breeds in America. Before he left England, he sired Ch. Perrancourt Playful who, up to 1996, was the breed record holder. He also sired Ch. Drakehall Debra of Junaken, the dam of many Champions, and Ch. Drakehall Diadem, dam of Crufts Supreme Champion, Ginger Xmas Carol. Brigand was Top Airedale in 1978.

For Prelude's third litter, a different

128

sire was chosen, Ch. Bengal Tarquin, who produced Ch. Bengal Turith Comet and Dan. Ch. Turith Commander, both these males also becoming top sires. Comet sired Am. Ch. Bravo True Grit and Am. Ch. Bravo Star Buck before he sadly died.

Litter four produced one of Judy's favourite dogs, Ch. Turith Echelon Of Saredon, sired by Am. Ch. Saredon Military Man. Echelon was exported to Carol Scott in America. Before leaving, he produced Ch. The Deerhunter Of Saredon and, in the US, one of his sons was Am. Ch. Bravo Ironman.

Prelude's last litter contained a bitch, Turith Feature, who was never a Champion but was the dam of Ch. Saredon The Jazzsinger.

Another Saredon bitch by Brigand, Ch. Saredon Brown Sugar, was mated to Saredon Sir Duke and produced a wonderful dog, Ch. Saredon Super Trooper. He was a Group winner and Top Airedale 1982 and Judy still thinks he was the best Airedale that she ever bred.

Then Duke surpassed himself yet again and from a bitch, Saredon Heartbreaker (a sister to Jazzsinger), produced Ch. Saredon Handyman. Handyman was Top Airedale for two years, a Group winner and the male breed record holder.

Jazzsinger and Handyman gave Judy two lines so she could breed Jazzsinger's offspring to Handyman's and vice versa. From these came many more Saredon Champions and a line of eight Champion males, as follows.
Line one: Military Man, Echelon, Deerhunter, Jazzsinger, Ballintober Gold Of Saredon, Saredon Start The Fire, Saredon Light The Fire, Saredon Lightning Strikes (Top Airedale 1998).
Line two: Saredon Sir Duke, who sired Saredon Super Trooper and Saredon Handyman.

The kennel's bitch strength came through Ch. S. The Jazzsinger, who sired Ch. S. September Morn. From her, came Ch. S. Sweet Caroline, who was mated to Ch. S. Light The Fire, producing Ch. S. Billie Jean and Ch. S.

Ch. Saredon Lightening Strikes: Top Airedale 1998.

Photo: David Dalton.

Jennifer Eccles, plus Top Winning Airedale of 1998 and 99, Ch. Saredon Lightning Strikes.

SHADLIAN – Jan Favell and Keith Raper

From a very early age Jan was surrounded by dogs of many breeds, but decided upon an Airedale as a family dog. Millie Kington of Searchlight Airedales knew of a litter by her stud dog. Jan selected a dog puppy 'Benson', better known later as Janber Mr Rinjee. Benson won Junior Dog at the Airedale Terrier Centenary Show in 1976 (the first of many wins) – and Jan was hooked!

She bought a bitch from the Saredon kennel with the appropriate qualities to begin a breeding programme with Janber Mr Rinjee. The bitch was Turith Baroness, litter sister to Ch. Turith Brigand (Ch. Siccawei Galliard x Prelude Of Turith). She produced many Championship Show-winning puppies and set Jan on her way to a successful breeding and showing kennel under the affix of Shadli (the first two letters of her children's names, SHaun, ADrian and LIsa).

She then purchased Tintara Arctos who had the Siccawei bloodlines that Jan was looking for. The first Champion was Shadli Adorn (Wellington of Lyonsdown of Searchlight x Shadli Party Piece). The next was Shadli Classy Charmer (Ch. Siccawei Galliard x Shadli Party Piece), who was top winning bitch in 1984 while in the ownership of Herr W. Schonenberg, and was handled by Kevin Brown to nine CCs and BoB. Shadli Party Piece was shown only lightly but produced Champions and many show-winning Airedales. Jan went on to breed

many more Champions in subsequent years.

She also exported dogs, some as Champions, others who became Champions in their new homelands. Ch. Shadli Fantom (Ch. Jokyl Gallipants x Ch. Shadli Classy Charmer) went to the USA as an English Champion and later, after his American Championship sired many quality puppies. Other dogs went to USA, Canada, Japan, Italy, Denmark and Germany. During 1988, Shadli Manipulator At Jokyl ('Nip') and Shadli Lord Luke both gained their Italian Championships and were battling in first and second places for the honour of top Airedale in Italy. Around the same time, Lord Luke's litter brother 'Matt' (Eng. Ch. Shadli Likely Lad) went to live in Denmark where he attained his Danish Championship and was top Airedale.

Jan always trimmed her own dogs and prepared them for shows. In 1997 she was asked to do a trimming demonstration for NEATC and helped and advised newcomers on trimming.

She is a Championship Show judge and awards Airedale CCs and has been invited to judge the regular classes in April 2000 at the Specialty show of the Airedale Terrier Club of Metropolitan Washington in the USA, her first overseas judging appointment.

Since 1993, Jan and her new partner Keith Raper have built a successful breeding/showing kennel under the affix Shadlian. Their first true Shadlian Airedale was Shadlian Uessay (Sally): she now has one CC, four Reserve CCs, one BoB and two BIS. In 1997, as a puppy, she went BIS at the Airedale Terrier Club of Scotland Open Show. She returned in 1998 to repeat that success, the following day attaining her first CC and BoB at the Scottish Kennel Club Championship Show to complete a Scottish double.

In May 1999, Sally produced her first litter (five puppies) via artificial insemination from an American dog, Am. Ch. Highpoint's Dakota. This was the first time artificial insemination has been used in Airedales in the UK.

The first dog campaigned after Keith and Jan joined forces was Tessie (Shadli Temptress). She attained several RCCs and two BIS and has now retired from the show ring. She has produced a super litter by Shadlian Red Sox, maintaining the bloodlines so carefully developed over the years.

In Tessie's first litter was a fine upstanding young man, Jake, who went on to become the canine hero of the Disney movie 101 Dalmatians and is now living in luxury with his animal trainer on a ranch in Florida.

In the Shadlian kennel particular attention is paid to the early socialisation of puppies, partly to address temperament problems in the Airedale ring in recent years.

STARGUS – Lesley and Gus Lee
After 23 years in the breed, the Lees look back fondly to their first dog – Ch. Stargus Sea King. 'Dickon' was an all-round composite male of good type, conformation, temperament and showmanship. The judge's critique at Crufts 1987 said of Dickon: "His character is outstanding and I had no hesitation in awarding him the CC. Lovely coat and colour, head with balance, good expression from dark eye to correct ear carriage, has strength in neck and shoulders, carries good depth

Ch. Stargus War Lord.
Photo: Steph Holbrook.

in body, has well boned legs and good feet, level topline with good tail carriage, strong quarters, sound in movement, the whole beautifully presented." The judge on the day was the late Gerry Howells (Cortella), breed specialist and one-time chairman of the UK parent club. Dickon in normal stance stood twenty-three and a half inches at the shoulder but when showing he was always on the 'tip-toe of expectation'.

Dickon's major wins include 15 CCs, 15 Reserve CCs, double junior warrant winner, triple Gold Medal winner, and six BIS including National Airedale Terrier Association and Midland Counties Airedale Terrier Association.

Eng. Am. Ch. Florac King Of Scots: A top winner and an influential sire. One of his most famous sons is Am. Ch. Serendipity's Eagle's Wings. Photo: Holloway.

He won his title at Crufts 1986 before he was two years old, and his tenth CC at Crufts 1987. He was second in the Terrier Group on two occasions at All Breed General Championship shows, at Birmingham and Bournemouth. He was seventeen times BoB. He left his indelible mark on his progeny, one of whom, after a meteoric UK show career, went to the USA – Eng. Ch. Florac King Of Scots At Stargus.

'Scot', in his short time on the UK circuit, won three CCs with BoB and BIS at the South of England Airedale Terrier Club, junior warrant and two Gold Medals, as well as multiple BoB and BIS at open level. Scot is very hard to fault. From eight weeks of age, he had the necessary show attitude and the 'look of eagles'. Another composite male, fractionally under 24 inches at the shoulder, he dominated the ring. In the USA, Scot went on to become a multiple BIS winner and top sire. One of his offspring is the top winning Airedale of all time, Am. Ch. Serendipity Eagle's Wings.

Scot also sired the Crufts 1992 BoB, Stargus Kings Highlander. A winner of two CCs with BoB, he was never to gain his title. 'King' sired Ch. City Slicker Of Stargus who, after gaining his English title and having a great run of wins including Groups on the Irish circuit, went to the USA where he became Champion and then added 'International' to his titles.

From a King Of Scots' daughter, Stargus Queen Of Scots, who was bred to Ch. Tintara Royal Salute, the kennel had a slightly different type – smaller, cobbier, but very much carrying the Sea King/Scot temperament and showmanship. The dog puppy kept by the Lees became Ch. Stargus Law Lord, who was shown in tandem with City Slicker. 'Oliver', was also successful on the Irish circuit. He had a beautiful head and the most wonderful ear-carriage with thin leathers, a lovely arched neck into shoulders, a good topline and tailset, and good rear angulation. Oliver was bred to Saredon Socialite (a Sea King daughter) and from this the kennel kept Ch. Stargus War Lord, who won 15 CCs and 15 reserve CCs, equalling Sea King's record, and winning the Crufts CC and BoB in 1995 and the CC again in 1996. 'Jason' was also Top Male in 1995. He was the stamp of his sire but had a slightly better front – a lovely dog to show and handle and to look at from all angles.

From Jason came a beautiful bitch, War Of The Roses, a winner of two reserve CCs who has been admired by many. Both Oliver and Jason went on to great success on the Continental show circuit. A repeat mating of Law Lord to Socialite produced Ch. Stargus Shoot To Kill. This dog is really hard to fault; though on the small side, he is wonderfully balanced, with a super outline. He was also a Group placement at several shows. 'Shooter' went to Denmark and is now Danish, Swedish, and International Champion. While in the UK, Shooter sired some very promising puppies, one of whom was best puppy at Crufts 1998

– McKerros The Laird Of Stargus. Shooter was bred to American import Terrydale Matter Of Time For Stargus and produced Stargus Sharpshooter, who won many BPIS as well as CC and reserve CC. Thanks to Sharpshooter's wins, together with the winning puppies from other kennels, Shooter was awarded Top Sire 1997.

King Creole Of Stargus was the last dog sired by Sea King in the Stargus kennel, a great character who certainly loves life to the full. 'Elvis' recently went to the USA where he quickly gained his American title, but he did leave the Lees with two lovely sons. They are Ch. Tebross Kings Advocate for Stargus, the winner of eight CCs and BIS at the UK parent club's prestigious National Airedale Terrier Championship Show, and the youngster Stargus Devil In Disguise.

TINTARA – Pat Crome
While living in Australia, Pat applied for and got a school holiday job at the Hillmere Kennels owned by Misses Eila and Lorna Green (later Mrs Lorna Schuster). On returning to England, she purchased her first bitch in 1954 for the then enormous sum of twelve guineas! The puppy was from the Riverina kennels of the late Pat MacCaughey and Max Schuth and was a litter sister to Ch. Riverina Tweed, sire of the famous Ch. Riverina Tweedsbairn. Sadly, her career was cut short as the result of a road accident.

Pat next acquired Riverina Radiance (Ch. Riverina Siccawei Phoebus x Ch. Riverina Encore). Mated to Riverina Furore, Radiance produced Pat's first litter in 1957. Two bitch pups were run on with minor success, then, in 1961,

Ch. Tintara Quickstep: Winner of three CCs and BIS at a breed Ch. show.

Pat purchased Riverina Rosemarie of Tintara (Ch. Riverina Tweedsbairn x Raimon Ragtime), the foundation of the current line.

Pat's second litter, sired by Ch. Bengal Fastnet, produced the kennel's first Champion, Ch. Tintara Classical, who gained her crown at Crufts 1967. 'Classical' produced two Champions, Ch. Tintara Mulberry (made up in 1972, sired by Siccawei Andros) and Ch. Tintara Pennyroyal, made up in 1974 and winner of Terrier Group Two the same year – her sire was Ch. Siccawei Kings Ransom.

'Pennyroyal' was mated to Ch. Siccawei Galliard. A dog was kept from this litter and became Eng. Int. Ch.

Tintara Trustee. Trustee won BPIS All Breeds at Richmond Championship Show in 1975, the following year gaining his title and also becoming Best Dog in Show at the celebrated Airedale Centenary Show in 1976.

Tintara Persephone (who was litter sister to Pennyroyal) mated to Ch. Jokyl Smart Guy produced Ch. Tintara Upstart who was made up 1978. Trustee and Upstart produced Ch. Tintara Zealous, made up in 1979, and winning BIS All Breeds and Terrier Group at South Wales Kennel Association Championship Show the same year. Ch. Tintara Quickstep (Jokyl Smart Set x Tintara Icando) won three CCs and nine reserve CCs, with a BIS at a breed

Championship Show. Icando also produced the next Champion, Ch. Tintara Royal Salute, sired by Ch Saredon The Jazzsinger. Taking his title in 1991, he also won a BIS at a breed Championship Show. During his show career he gained six CCs, seven reserve CCs and five BoBs. 'Quickstep' produced Ch. Tintara Unity At Jokyl born in 1992 and sired by Ch. Jokyl Gallipants. The latest Champion, born in 1995, is Ch. Tintara Waltz Time, sired by Ch. Jokyl Lucky Strike. Unity was made up in 1994 and has to her credit eight CCs and ten reserve CCs, and BIS at a breed Championship Show. Waltz Time to date has won seven CCs, six reserve CCs, four

BoB, Terrier Group Two, BIS and three reserve BIS.

Pat has shown and/or bred ten UK Champions as well as numerous overseas and International Champions, not forgetting Irish Champion, Tintara Firethorn, campaigned by Martin and Sue Kealy. Since her first Championship judging appointment in 1969, Pat has judged 15 UK shows, one being Crufts Centenary 1991, and in ten countries at Championship level.

In the Tintara breeding programme, Riverina, Bengal and Siccawei blood figures significantly, resulting in elegant Airedales which maintain the quality, character and type of the breed.

Ch. Tintara Waltz Time: Winner of eight CCs to date. Photo: Steph Holbrook.

11 AIREDALES IN NORTH AMERICA
By Mareth Kipp

USA

The American Airedale as we now know him is still the same dog we knew 25 years ago, only different. He is still black and tan, still a protector of hearth and home, still hunts, still participates in Obedience and Agility and still competes in the show ring. We have seen the size of the Airedale increase, and we have seen it decrease. We have seen ears go from being highly set back to the proper and accepted Airedale ear.

One thing we are still seeing in the American show ring is the Airedale best described as 'elegant'. Although it is a departure from the Standard as we know it, these are the dogs currently doing the majority of winning. It seems the Airedale that is shorter on leg and heavier-bodied is currently out of vogue. Trends will always show up in the ring

Opposite page: Can. Ch. Paradym So Surreal, bred by Kelly Wood.
The all-round Airedale Terrier has made his mark in the show ring, competing in Obedience, Agility, and as a highly-valued companion.

and then in the whelping box. The current winner is often the benchmark that many breeders aspire to. But the Airedale is the Airedale is the Airedale, and to understand his history is to be able to predict his future.

The Airedale's heritage is deeply rooted in the Aire valley in England. From the first imported dog to the present time, English dogs have played an important role in the development of the American Airedale. During the past 25 years, we have seen a number of dogs imported to this country. These dogs include, but are not limited to, Ch. Jokyl Superman and his son Ch. Jokyl Supermaster, Ch. Jokyl Prince Regent, Ch. Turith Adonis, Ch. Turith Echelon Of Saredon, Bengal Turith Comet and Ch. Florac King Of Scots At Stargus. These dogs have gone on to produce offspring that have continued to play an important part of the development of the dog we see in the ring today.

SUPERMAN AND SUPERMASTER
Ch. Jokyl Superman arrived in America in the late 1960s and hit the ground running. He won numerous Specialties,

Groups and a Best in Show. He was a smaller dog by today's standards, closer to 23 ins than to 24 ins, compact, and full of himself. He was a great show dog, piloted by the talented Bill Thompson. He proved to be a good producer, siring many Champions including both Group and Specialty winners. His offspring also went on to become top producers as well. His first American Champion was Ch. Moraine Bright Promise, a top winner as well as a producer of 13 Champion get herself. Superman was also the sire of Ch. Harbor Hills Klark Kent and Ch. Harbor Hills Lois Lane, both winners and producers as well. He was an important foundation sire for many of today's current Airedale breeders and exhibitors.

Following the arrival of Superman, Stone Ridge Kennel of Illinois imported his son, Jokyl Supermaster, in November 1970. Supermaster's dam was Ch. Jokyl Queen Of Space, a Ch. Jokyl Benal Figaro daughter. Figaro's pedigree helped American breeders to access another strand of the English bloodlines.

Janet Johnson Framke described Supermaster thus: "To best describe him would be to see his value as a stud dog. He was a short-backed, cobby dog with a good wire coat, movement and a super tail-set. While many would fault his full head, it was in balance with his body. The show ring was never his favorite place to spend time. When he was being gaited around the ring, as he approached the entry gate, he would pull to leave the ring. Despite his obvious dislike for the show ring, he was an Airedale Terrier Club of America Bowl winner. He won the Ohio Specialty as well as a hard-fought Best in Show (BIS).

The foundation bitches for Stone Ridge came from the then very popular Benaire Kennel, also located in Illinois. The Benaire bitches had great coat and color, long heads and the longer bodies to accompany them. They needed improvement in tail-sets. The cross with Supermaster achieved this. He shortened backs, improved tail-sets and movement. The offspring were able to keep the long heads and great red and black color of their dams.

Supermaster was also bred to Ch. Bengal Springtime to produce Ch. Eden's Spring Hepatica, the sire of the very popular American Airedale, Ch. Eden's Sal Sorbus. Supermaster was also the sire and grandsire of other Bowl winners as well as multiple Group winners. Supermaster became a top producing Airedale and had a truly important role in improving the breed in both the United States and Canada.

THE PRELUDE LINE

To fully understand the impact of English dogs on the future of the American Airedale, one has to look at the great producing bitch, Prelude Of Turith. As the saying goes, behind every great man is a woman. The same can be said of Prelude, who appears in more American pedigrees than any other bitch in recent history.

She may not appear in the first couple of generations, but her influence is there through her sons, the first being Ch. Turith Adonis, followed by litter brothers Ch. Turith Country Cousin and Bengal Turith Comet. From her next litter came Ch. Turith Echelon Of Saredon, the third Prelude son to have a strong influence on American pedigrees.

FREDDY

To best describe Ch. Turith Adonis I contacted his handler Peter Green. Peter first saw 'Freddy' at the Ladies' Kennel Association Show in England. Judy Averis had purchased him from Beryl Blower, a breeder of both Airedales and Welsh Terriers. Peter immediately knew that Freddy was a dog that American breeders needed in their breeding programs. Peter left him there to be made an English Champion, but, for whatever reason that was not immediately accomplished, and Peter imported Freddy lacking his third Challenge Certificate.

Freddy made his debut in America during the terrier 'Show of Shows' – Montgomery County weekend. He went Best of Breed (BoB) at the highly competitive Hatboro Kennel Club Show under terrier authority Robert Moore. He was Best of Winners at Devon and, in the pouring rain of Montgomery County Kennel Club, he again went Best of Breed under another terrier authority, AnneMarie Moore. He went on to win four consecutive breeds at Montgomery, as well as at the Westminster Kennel Club Show. He won over 50 Groups but was awarded only one BIS, under the very highly regarded William Kendrick. Freddy was a true terrier and loved other Airedales and terriers, but was generally very bored with the BIS line-up. During his entire American career, he was only defeated twice in the breed.

Freddy played a very important role as a stud dog, both in England and in America. He sired the top winning Ch. Perrancourt Playful in England. She was England's Dog of the Year in 1979. His grand-daughter, the bitch Ch. Ginger Xmas Carol, achieved Dog of the Year

award in 1985. She was also the Crufts Best in Show winner in 1986. In America, his top winning daughter, Ch. Moraine Promises To Keep, went on to be a top show dog as well as a strong producer. Freddy's strength seemed to be in producing high-quality bitches. There seemed to be the feeling that he could improve on almost every bitch he was bred to. There are still many lines in both England and America that owe their success to Ch. Turith Adonis.

COMET

Bengal Turith Comet arrived in America and was picked up to be shown by the world-famous Ric Chashoudian. As luck would have it, Ric had a bitch in season and he determined she was the right choice for Comet. Her name was Ch. Bravo Bonanza Belle DeAAA, a great show dog and producer in her own right. Unfortunately, that was the only litter Comet would produce in America as he died a few days later. The litter produced two of America's most popular and successful stud and show dogs, Ch. Bravo True Grit and Ch. Bravo Star Buck.

THE BRAVO BOYS

In addition to True Grit and Star Buck, there were two other males that finished their Championship as well, making this only breeding an important one for the future of Airedales in America. No two dogs have made as much impact on the Airedale breed as True Grit and Star Buck. The former won BIS at Montgomery County Kennel Club in 1981.

To paraphrase Ric Chashoudian, these two dogs were as different as day and night. True Grit, whose call name was

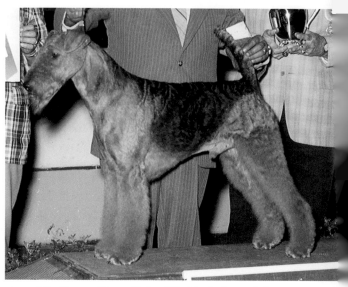

Am. Ch. Bravo Star Buck: Competed at the highest level, and went on to sire 76 Champions.

Am. Ch. Bravo True Grit: Highly influential in the show ring and as a sire.

'Toby', was cobby, a thinker and the extrovert. Star Buck or 'Duke' to his friends, was reachy, taller, cunning, the bully, and an introvert. That the brothers were 'highly visible' goes without saying. Both dogs enjoyed success at the highest level, often in direct competition with each other. The pair were presented by highly qualified and talented handlers, Toby by Ric Chashoudian and Duke by Clay Cody. When they were together in the ring it was electrifying. Neither dominated the other. Each had his own strengths and followers. Occasions when they were in the ring together brought the audience to its feet. It would be impossible to complete their line of Champion descendants.

As sires, Ch. Bravo True Grit and Ch. Bravo Star Buck have proven their worth. Toby sired 76 Champions and Duke sired 68. Many of their get have gone on to be top winners and producers as well.

Duke left a great legacy in America, siring many top-winning dogs including Ch. Blackjack's Mighty Sampson. Sampson sired Ch. Blackjack's Nostradamus. Nostradamus returned to England and did a respectable amount of winning and producing there as well. Another Specialty winner sired by Duke was Ch. Tartan Oil Patch Star, herself a breed winner at the Montgomery County Kennel Club Show.

A strong line featuring Duke developed through many of the Safari-bred dogs. A grandson, Ch. Highpoints Dakota, was a consistent winner during 1996 and 1997. Dakota has several get making a name and impact on the breed in the show ring.

Toby's most famous top-winning and producing son was Ch. Finlair Tiger Of Stone Ridge. Until recently, he was the all-time top winner as well as being one of the top breed producers. Just as Toby had a popular and productive brother, so did Tiger. His brother was Ch. Finlair Lyon Of Stone Ridge. Although Lyon was not shown as often as Tiger or used as frequently, he made an impact on several kennels in America.

TIGER AND LYON

The two Bravo brothers were alike, only different, and so were the Finlair boys. Tiger was cobby, and of average size. He carried more grizzle than black and tan, and had a pair of very high-set ears. His head was not his strongest asset. However, in the ring with ears set the way they were, he was magnificent. Tiger never entered a show ring he did not like, nor encountered a crowd he could not win over. He had the perfect temperament. He was a great show dog and an easy, loving house dog. He truly was one of those great mixtures of show and pet.

Tiger's top winning son was Am. and Can. Ch. Moraine Hold That Tiger. 'Terry', a multiple BIS winner, lived in Canada for the majority of his life. He made an impact on many Canadian Airedales, as well as producing Champion offspring in the US. Terry continues to have an impact on breeding programs in both countries.

Ch. Finlair Tiger of Stone Ridge was the top winning BIS Airedale from 1984 until 1996, with 25 Best in Shows. This record was broken in 1996 by his great-great grandson, Ch. Serendipity's Eagle's Wings. In addition to his 25 BIS, Tiger won 81 Groups and three Airedale Terrier Club of America National Specialties. The last time he won was at eight and a-half years from the Veterans

Am. Ch. Finlair Tiger Of Stone Ridge: Top winning BIS Airedale from 1984 to 1996, with 25 Best in Shows.

Am. Ch. Moraine Hold That Tiger: A top winning son of Am. Ch. Finlair Tiger Of Stoneridge.

Class at Montgomery County Kennel Club. Tiger was a joy to watch in the ring. He stood his own ground, willing to make love or war. He stared down at his opposition. Tiger proved that a correct outline, with correct angles, great attitude and proper movement can and did exist in one animal. As one would expect from a dog bred as royally as he was, he is still tied with his sire, Ch. Bravo True Grit, as all-time top producing sire with 76 American Champions.

Tiger's brother Lyon was more up on leg, not quite as cobby and carried a longer head. He also sported a darker jacket than Tiger, but never really enjoyed the show ring as much as his brother.

Not to be outdone by the two brothers, another younger Toby son, Ch. Finlair Imperial Trent, made an impact on the breed as well. Trent finished his Championship at the world-famous Westminster Kennel Club Show. He was never shown to the extent that Tiger was, but nevertheless was a top-ten Airedale in 1987 as well as a Specialty winner. He was as different from Tiger as Lyon was. Trent was a long-legged dog. He carried more height then length of back. He had a long neck, and a long, full face, set off with a pair of fancy ears. He moved with ease and grace, carrying himself around the ring with a presence that begged you to look at him. His strength, like that of his brothers, was as a stud dog. He became the foundation for several breeders in the Kansas area as well as being responsible for many Champion get in future generations.

In addition to the boys from Finlair, Ch. Bravo True Grit produced another top-producing son, Ch. Epoch's Nineteen Eighty-Four. 'Orwell', as he was called, sired both sweepstake and Specialty winners. His son, Ch. Darbywood Preferred Stock, was exported to Denmark where he was the top Airedale in 1995 and 1996. A Toby grandson, Int. Ch. M.J.'s Stone Ridge Chosen One, has had an impact on the Airedale breed around the world, including producing Champion offspring in the US, Germany and Australia.

FINLAIR ISIS
Following Tiger in the Specials ring came his full sister, Ch. Finlair Isis. As a show dog she dominated the Airedale world. She won 11 BIS, was awarded 51 Group Firsts and six Airedale Terrier Club of America National Specialties. As a youngster 'Na-Bi' was like a fawn or thoroughbred filly. She had more angles then Tiger. Although she was slightly

more upright in the shoulder, she moved perfectly in the front. Her head was cleaner in the skull with a longer foreface, but she did not have as flat topskull planes as Tiger. She carried her head and neck more upright and elegantly than Tiger's more forward-leaning look. Na-Bi's tail-set and carriage were perfect. Her tail seldom needed to be held up even for photos. Her size, bone and substance made it easy for her to compete against the males without ever looking masculine. Na-bi had correct but fancy ears that helped her expression. She was not blessed with great body coat, but grew tremendous amounts of good leg and facial hair. She was the consummate show dog, moving around the ring on a loose lead, always exhibiting strength, elegance and coordination. There was so much to like about her – and she made many friends for the Airedale while she was being campaigned. Na-bi continues to hold the record as the top winning bitch in the United States.

When bred, Na-Bi produced Ch. Finlair Scottshire Mako. Mako is the sire of Am. Can. Ch. Paradyn So Surreal. She is a Specialty-winning bitch in both the US and Canada. She is the top winning Specialty winner for Airedales in Canada. When she ventured 'south of the border', she served notice to American breeders that she could win at Specialties there as well. It would be many years before another Airedale would do the kind of winning that either Tiger or Na-Bi achieved.

ECHELON AND LADY
Ch. Turith Echelon Of Saredon arrived in America in the 1980s and spent the majority of his life in California. He had a great show career and was the sire of numerous Champions. Many Scottshire-bred dogs have Echelon as part of their pedigree.

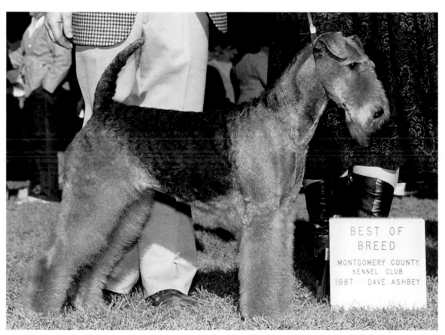

Am. Ch. Finlair Isis: This bitch dominated the show world at the height of her career.

Ashbey Photography.

Am. Ch. Terrydale's Adorable Lady: Dam of Am. Ch. Terrydale Int'l Affair.

Another strong female line was established when a Tiger of Stone Ridge daughter, Ch. Terrydale's Adorable Lady, a National Specialty and BIS winner in her own right, was bred to Ch. Brisline's Lady's Man. One of the puppies resulting from this litter, would prove to be Lady's greatest legacy. His name was Terrydale Int'l Affair.

FELIX

To best understand the story of Felix (Int'l Affair), let his best friend and handler Maripi Wooldridge tell the story: "Everything about Felix has been a combination of need, luck and destiny. Twice his dam was bred to True Grit and missed. On her next heat, she was sent to California to be bred to Ch. Brisline's Lady's Man. As luck would have it, she conceived. Around the time Felix was eight months old, Terry Clark

(Terrydale) and I went to England and fell in love with a young dog named Florac King Of Scots At Stargus and were fortunate enough to purchase him.

"Since Felix was a totally different type than what I liked (short on leg), I decided to sell him. He went to Mexico, hence the name Int'l Affair. Because of the Mexican economy at the time, he was never fully paid for and thus the papers were never transferred. The Terrydale breeding program needed a linebred dog to use with the Scot daughters and the search for Felix was on. Unbelievably, he was found at a kennel 45 minutes from where he was born and raised. He finally returned home at five years of age with chronic ear and gum infections, but also with his tail wagging and a totally forgiving heart. As people's priorities tend to change, so did the Clarks'. They decided to get out of dogs and I had the chance to buy Felix back. And, as they say, the rest is history. He is a perfect gentleman, never starts a fight, and has proven to be the perfect companion."

For those Airedalers lucky enough to have seen him, especially in the Veterans classes, Felix is a joy to behold. He carries a wonderfully hard jacket, still has a clean, long head with perfect ears and never quits showing. His puppies are not hard to spot. The combination of Scot daughters to Felix has proven to be successful for many American breeders. Int'l Affair has been a very prolific sire and puts his stamp on his get. They resemble him a great deal, with lovely heads and a perfect eye. By many standards, they could use a bit more leg, but watching them go around the ring is poetry in motion.

As a ten-year-old veteran, he won BoB at the Montgomery County Kennel Club show in 1998, as well as a hotly contested Group 2. He was also BoB at the very prestigious Westminster Kennel Club Show in 1999. One of his greatest winning sons, Ch. Spindletop New Kid in Town, also a Scot grandson, is a multiple Group and Specialty winner as well.

Another True Grit grandson, Ch. Cripple Creek George Burns, was very successful in the breed ring, including several appearances as a veteran. He is the sire of BIS winning, Ch. Timberwyck Wild Bill Cody.

Though these dogs had their heyday in the 1980s and into the 1990s, their influence on the breed continues to this day.

Eng. Am. Ch. Florac King Of Scots At Stargus: An influential import from the UK.

SCOT

As we have discovered, many of the pedigrees of the top winners and producers include some of the same dogs. To this end, we introduced another English dog into the gene pool. Ch. Florac King Of Scots At Stargus arrived early in the 1990s. He would also prove to have a great effect on the breed. He was a dog that caused much comment in Airedale circles. He was quite extreme for many American fanciers. He had a long head with tremendous foreface. Some would say that his ears were not his fortune. Although set on top of his head, they did not carry the lift that many American breeders and judges were used to seeing. His show career did not include the Group, Specialty and BIS wins of some of the other Airedales, but his impact as a stud dog cannot be denied.

In talking to his current owner and handler, Maripi Wooldridge, we learn

Am. Ch. Terrydale Int'l Affair: A great winner, even in his tenth year. Ashbey Photography.

145

some of the things that made Scot a friend as well as show dog. She says he was the hardest and most difficult dog she ever had to deal with, but he is still part of her household at the age of 13. He watches over his home and yard with the interest of a typical Airedale. He will poke and bark at anything new and is a good judge of human character. Maripi adds that Scot has a definite and distinctive personality – demanding, giving, serious, funny, a beast and pumpkin all at once.

Scot's real legacy is in his offspring. He sired many Champions as well as loving companions. It is expected that, before the next decade, he will surpass all other sires as the top producer of Champion Airedales. He did not necessarily stamp his offspring with his physical attributes, but he always seemed to bring out the best in the bitches he was bred to.

DINAH
This chapter of Airedales in America would be incomplete if it did not include Ch. Coppercrest Dinah. Dinah was a great show dog and loved the ring. She was a top winner for the Coppercrest kennel of June and Robin Dutcher. As a BoB winner at the Montgomery County Kennel Club Show, she made it possible for people to believe that Airedale bitches can win the big shows.

A RECORD BREAKER
In more recent years, the top winning Airedale in the country was Ch. Serendipity's Eagle's Wings. Peter, as he was called, broke every existing show record for Airedales in this country. He was top Airedale for 1994 through 1996 and top Airedale sire for 1997. It is interesting to note that he too has strong links to his English cousins. He is sired by Ch. Florac King Of Scots At Stargus and is a great-grandson of Ch. Bravo True Grit.

Peter had a presence in the show ring that seemed to develop the longer he was in there. He had a quiet quality about him. He was not one to be aggressive

Am. Ch. Moraine Where Eagles Dare: A son of Am. Ch. Serendipity's Eagle's Wings, now living in Argentina.

Booth Photography.

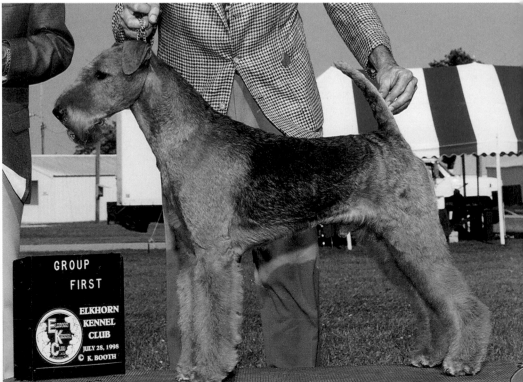

GROUP FIRST

ELKHORN KENNEL CLUB JULY 28, 1998 © K. BOOTH

when he was being shown, but was always the perfect gentleman. He was an easy dog to like, and all Airedale – up on leg, great coat, short back and bang-on tail-set, along with a beautiful head and ears. He was a fluid mover, at a time when movement was not the greatest feature of many Airedales. As one would hope from a dog that seemed to have been bred to be a sire, he has already produced over a dozen Champions. Among those dozen were several Specialty winners, including the multiple Group winner, Ch. Moraine Where Eagles Dare. This youngster is now in Argentina and looks forward to making an impact on breeding programs there as well.

THE BREED TODAY

With the advent of affordable airfares more Airedales were sent to different parts of the country to be bred. Prior to that, the majority of the dogs on either coast and in the Midwest all seemed to have their own unique similarities as well as differences. The dogs on the West Coast tended to have a bit more leg under them; the East Coast dogs were a bit shorter in back. The dogs in the Midwest were also a bit shorter in back and not up on leg. Other than the larger Specialties, few people were able to view the results of breeding programs in other parts of the country. For many reasons, the large kennels faded from the picture and responsibility for the continuation of the breed fell to the smaller breeder. Pockets developed within the country where smaller kennels flourished. They can still be found in Southern California, the San Francisco area, around the Chicago-Illinois area and up and down the East Coast.

As interest in the breed seemed to grow, more local Airedale clubs were formed. We now have Specialty clubs in most parts of the United States, from Massachusetts to Illinois, Minnesota, Northern and Southern California and many states in between. It was encouraging to see that, as some of the older Airedale breeders had to cut back on their breeding programs, younger and equally eager breeders were there to take their place. We now recognize names such as White Rose, Bristol Aire, Serendipity, Terrydale, Spindletop, Epoch, D'Aire, Stone Ridge, Darbywood, Moraine, Brisline, Terrorific, Tartan and, of course, the many other breeders who consistently produce dogs of quality.

SUMMARY

The popularity of Airedales in America has seen its highs and its lows. It is not the desire of the majority of Airedale owners to see this breed climb to the number one spot in registrations by the American Kennel Club. We all know that with popularity come the inherent problems of over-producing and mass-production. Airedales currently rank in about 50th position as far as registrations go. For serious breeders and fanciers, that suits everyone just fine.

To know the true personality of an Airedale is a unique thing. He is not for everyone and should not be placed without careful consideration. He is a very special breed of dog – alert, headstrong, intelligent, independent, handsome, a clown and most of all, a terrific member of his family. We will continue to look to his roots and his heritage to further his development. Yes, the Airedale is alive and well in the USA!

CANADA
by Margaret A. Saltzmann

Airedales are shown in reasonable numbers on the East Coast of Canada. Most shows have entries of two to six, with All Breed Terrier Specialties bringing numbers in the high teens or low twenties. The Atlantic Provinces have several breeders, not all of whom are active in show rings but whose dogs are seen in the rings with some regularity. Given their numbers, Airedales do their share of winning, with many Group firsts as well as the occasional BIS. These dogs are also competitive elsewhere, often seen on the eastern seaboard of the US and occasionally in Central Canada.

TOP AIREDALES IN CANADA
The top five winning Airedales, and the number of points achieved in the show ring over a period of one year while being shown in Canada, are as follows.

1998: Top Airedale was Ch. Oakrun's Blue Jay Of Paradym with 681 points; in second place was Ch. Rollingstone's Unknown Legend with 430 points; third was Ch. Northcote No More Heartache with 226 points; fourth Ch. Cooleamber Brickberry Special with 216 points; and fifth was Ch. Regalridge Dior with 194 points.
1997: Top Airedale was Ch. Fairwood Mystique Tiger with 575 points; in second place Ch. Paradym Red Rebel, 555 points; third was Ch. Alpenaire's Healing Touch, 526 points; fourth Ch. Regalridge's Piece O' The Rock, 396 points; and in fifth place Ch. Aerie's Count Basie with 145 points.
1996: Top Airedale was Ch. Northcote

Can. Ch. Nanouska van't Asbroek: Top Airedale Terrier in 1992.

Aerie Alliance, 705 points; second Ch. Paradym So Surreal, 534 points; third Ch. Jefeica's High Voltage C, 492 points; fourth was Ch. Regalridge's Piece O' The Rock, 275; fifth was Ch. Harrington's You're So Vain with 203 points.
1995: Sixth Top Terrier and Top Airedale Ch. Fairewood Chrysanthemum Tiger-3, 119 points; second Ch. Bonaire Cymbeline Dress Code, 399 points; in third place Huntwood's Hollytroy Designer, 384 points; fourth place went to Ch. Windywalk's Mr Mugsy Malone, 305 points; and fifth was Ch. Regalridge's Marshall Dillon, 126 points.
1994: Top Terrier and Top Airedale, Ch. Fairewood Chrysanthemum Tiger with a total of 6,344 points; second Ch. Paradym Keep Me Posted, 634 points; third Ch. Lord Robin Of Kingaire, 358 points; fourth was Ch. Adalma's C.J. Morgan, 209 points; and fifth Ch. Shawndee Bulairo Hawk, 127 points.
1993: Seventh Top Terrier and Top Airedale Ch. Kingaire Cavalier Casey, 2,045 points; second Ch. Fairewood Chrysanthemum Tiger, 1,172 points; third Ch. Lord Robin Of Kingaire, 831

points; fourth place Ch. Paradym Keep Me Posted, 703 points; and fifth Ch. Regalridge Tartan North Star.
1992: Sixth Top Terrier and Top Airedale Ch. Nanouska van't Asbroek, 1,537 points; second Ch. Kingaire Cavalier Casey, 751 points; third was Ch. Regalridge Tartan North Star, 418 points; fourth Ch. Kingaire's Lord Ravenswood, 236 points; and fifth Ch. Fairewood Chrysanthemum Tiger.

PEDIGREE BREEDER OF THE YEAR

To receive this award, the breeder must breed at least three Champions within the set time limit of one year, which runs from July to June of the following year.

In 1998, three kennels won this prestigious award : Lydia Langley and Linda Smith of Bulairo kennels, Kelly Wood of Paradym kennels, and Jennifer Swan of the Ohsi kennels.

The previous year, 1997, saw Winnie Gervais of the Jalynaire Kennels, together with Carole Kane of Hollytroy kennels, accept the award.

In 1996, the award went to David R. O'Connor and Esther L. O'Connor of the Kingaire Kennels.

In 1995 and 1994, the award went to Kenneth C. Curren and Lee Stevens of the Regalridge Kennels.

Brian and Lotus Tutton took the award with Fairwood Airedales in 1993, and in 1992 it was Virginia Higdon of Ironcroft who won the award. Lee Stevens and Kenneth C. Curran of Regalridge took it in 1991.

HOLLYTROY – Carole Kane (co-owner Winnie Gervais).

Carole's fascination with Airedale Terriers began 20 years ago after she read a marvellous book written by the late Irene Hayes. Fifteen years would pass before Carole acquired her first show Airedales, a dog and bitch puppy out of Judy Averis's Saredon Cathy Song (Eng. Ch. Saredon Sir Duke x Eng. Ch. Saredon Brown Sugar). Frank Mayne of Westmayne Kennels in Nova Scotia had imported Cathy into Canada. The two puppies were named Holly and Troy, hence the kennel name Hollytroy.

Holly was not destined to be a producer of bitch puppies; rather she was known as a producer of big, handsome males. Eventually, Carole discontinued the line. Holly, now ten years old, still lives with her as a much-loved pet.

To start anew Carole decided to move into the more easily accessible American lines, thus Alanna, aka Am. Can. Ch. Huntwood's A Puppy For Dee (Am. Ch. Darbywood's Super Star x Am. Ch. Moraine Promise By Tiger), the

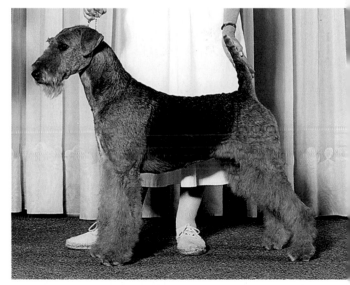

Am. Can. Ch. Huntwood's A Puppy For Dee, bred by Susan and Scott Kipp.

'sweetheart bitch' as she was called by other breeders, was to be her new beginning. All successes scored as a breeder can be directly attributed to Alanna, a dam of merit, and a producer par excellence. Scott and Susan Kipp of Wisconsin, USA, bred Alanna.

Alanna's first two litters produced seven top-notch Champions and several near things. Am. Can. Ch. Tartan Scottshire Cowboy sired Alanna's first litter. From this litter, she produced Ch. Hollytroy The Cowboy Connection and Ch. Hollytroy The Cowboy Way, as well as Winnie Gervais's Ch. Jalynaire Cowboy's Legacy and Am. Can. Ch. Jalynaire Dallas Cowboy

Bred to Am. Can. Ch. Huntwood's Hollytroy Designer for her second litter, Alanna produced Ch. Hollytroy Sydney MacGregor, Ch. Hollytroy The Designer's Touch, and Ch. Hollytroy Designer's Acclaim.

For Alanna's third and final litter she was bred to her grandsire, Am. Can. Ch. Moraine Hold That Tiger for what Carole believes to be her best homebred success to date, Ch. Hollytroy Tiger's Star Brite. 'Star' was shown only three times as an eleven-month-old and won three back-to-back Group Firsts and three BPIS.

Nearly every one of Alanna's Champion offspring has been awarded at least one Best Puppy in Show; all have multiple BoB, Group placements and Specialty wins to their credit. Alanna's greatest impact on the breed is that she produces absolute soundness and a temperament that is beyond reproach in her puppies.

At six years of age, Alanna has retired from the whelping box and is happy just to be Carole's companion.

HUGADALE – Margaret A. Saltzmann
Margaret says that her love of Airedales began in 1976 with her beloved Asco. It did not take long for her to realise that this dog did not know he was a dog but thought he was a person and behaved like a third child.

Asco was raised with Margaret's two boys, Klaus and Derk, who were four and seven years old at the time. Skiing, hockey, soccer, rafting on the waves in the ocean at Myrtle Beach or sailing on a Sun Fish in the lake – whatever the boys did, Asco did too. When he died in 1987 the family were all grief-stricken.

Margaret decided at this time to become involved in showing dogs, and found a wonderful Airedale she named Blazer. Blazer placed Best Puppy in Breed and won the Group 4 Puppy Sweeps at Credit Valley in December 1987; after that show, he collapsed.

At six months of age, Blazer had an adverse reaction to the rabies vaccine and at 11 months became so ill she thought she would lose him. The vet told her Blazer would not make it. She decided that he would, and did everything possible to make his life comfortable for as long as it would last with all the medications necessary. Her dreams of showing a dog seemed relatively unimportant compared with saving Blazer.

She did succeed in saving him and during those years decided to learn as much as possible about Airedales. She became a ringside observer and dog-show traveller without a dog. She met many wonderful Airedale breeders and owners during this time and made many new friends, which developed, into good, close friends, over the years.

Margaret's favourite shows are Crufts

Am. Can. Ch. Oakrun Beyond Myth V Hugdale, owned by Margaret Saltzmann.

and Montgomery. She took videos of all the shows she attended, analysing dog after dog. Blazer remained a constant companion and friend and despite many medical setbacks somehow always came back.

In 1996, Margaret decided to pursue the show ring once more. She found a lovely seven-week-old bitch called Glory. Blazer died in January, 1999.

Glory fulfilled Margaret's dream of rearing a show dog and finished her Canadian Championship on December 14th, 1997.

Just prior to gaining her title, she went Best of Breed out of the classes, under Judge Anne Rogers Clark at Brantford, Ontario.

Glory finished her American Championship on January 7th, 1998 at exactly 18 months of age with a 4 Point Major, going Best of Winners and Best of Opposite Sex. All wins to her American

Championship were Majors, with no minors.

In July 1998, Glory went on to win the Airedale Terrier Club of Canada's National Specialty, going Best of Breed and Best Canadian Bred under Judge Jon Cole from the USA.

In October 1998, Glory made the final cut and was one of the top ten finalists in the breed ring both at Hatboro, under Judge Robert Sharp, and at Devon, under Judge Ed Bivin. Her registered name is Am. Can. Ch. Oakrun Beyond Myth V Hugadale.

Glory is now a mother, with ten beautiful puppies sired by Am. Ch. Terrydale Int'l Affair. The litter was born on February 25th, 1999. Hugadale look forward to this being the start of many future Champions and wonderful Airedale companions for families who love the breed as much as Margaret does. Who says dreams do not come true?

PARADYM – Kelly Wood
It was after much research that Paradym Airedales acquired its foundation bitch 'Peggy', Am. Can. Ch. Ironcroft Priority Post, Am. CD, CDX, TT (Ch. Cymbeline Image Of Ironman x Ch. Ironcroft JP's Doin' Good). She was purchased from Marilyn Mincey of Cymbeline Airedales as a stud puppy back from a litter bred by Virginia Higdon (Ironcroft Airedales).

Peggy fulfilled her young breeder's dreams, not in the quantity of puppies produced (eleven in total from two litters), but in their quality, particularly in the litter sired by Am. Can. Ch. Moraine Hold That Tiger (Am. Ch. Finlair Tiger Of Stone Ridge x Moraine Chorus Line). Two litter sisters that resulted from this breeding have both made their mark here in Canada.

The first, Am. Can. Ch. Paradym Keep Me Posted, Am. Can. CD, or 'Mia', was twice an All-Breed Best in Show Winner, gained multiple Group firsts and other placements, was five times Best Puppy in Show, winner of the prestigious Puppy Of The Year tournament in 1993, and ranked as second Airedale in 1994. She was well known for her nice type, showy attitude and absolutely sound movement. She produced two litters, and, to date, she has five Champion offspring. From the litter sired by Am. Ch. Stone Ridge Fairewood Flyer CD, there were two significant winners. Am. Can. Ch. Paradym Red Rebel won many Terrier Group firsts and was Canada's second Top Airedale in 1997. His sister, Ch. Paradym Double Diamond, or 'Danta', won two Group placements en route to Championship, BoS and Best Puppy in Sweepstakes at the Airedale Terrier Club of Canada's National Specialty 1997 and won Winners Bitch, Best of Winners and BoS at the Airedale Terrier Club of Northern Ohio's Specialty in 1997.

Mia's litter sister 'Ginger', Am. Can. Ch. Paradym Post Parade, was Best in Specialty from the classes to finish her Championship at the ATCC National Specialty in 1993. Her strengths lay in her fabulous dark eye and expression, her length of neck and shortness of back. We have seen her head and eye expressed not only in her first and only litter (sired by Am. Ch. Finlair Scottshire Mako), but in the generation that was to follow as well. This one litter resulted in two Champions, one of whom is particularly notable. Am. Can. Ch. Paradym So Surreal, 'Dali', won at the ATCC National Specialty in 1996 and was second Airedale in Canada in 1996. Her most thrilling win was to be awarded BoS at the incomparable terrier show,

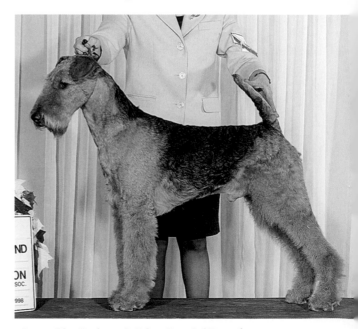

Can. Ch. Oakrun's Blue Jay Of Paradym:
Top winning Airedale in Canada in 1998.

Montgomery County, in 1996 (she had been Reserve Winners Bitch there the year before). She was Winners Bitch, Best of Winners and Best of Opposite Sex at Devon 1995, with multiple Group firsts and other placements.

Dali's young son, sired by the record-breaking BIS Airedale and Montgomery County BoB 1996, Am. Ch. Serendipity's Eagle's Wings, is Can. Ch. Oakrun's Blue Jay Of Paradym) or 'Jay'. Jay was co-bred and co-owned with John Voortman of Oakrun Airedales. At under two years of age, he is already proving himself worthy of his heritage. He is Top Airedale in Canada for 1998. A proud stallion-like dog, he has earned several Terrier Group firsts and two All-Breed Best Puppy in Shows, ATC Specialty Best of Opposite Sex 1998, ATC Northern Ohio Best in Sweepstakes, Steel Valley ATC Best in Sweepstakes, Reserve Winners Dog Devon 1998, in very limited showing. We expect him to be the one to thrill us for some time yet!

PARADYM CHAMPIONS
Foundation Bitch: Am. Can. Ch. Ironcroft Priority Post, Am. CD, Can. CDX, TT (Ch. Cymbeline Image Of Ironman x Ch. Ironcroft JP's Doin' Good)
1a) Can. Ch. Paradym Washington Post (d) (by Ch. Alpenaire's Matinee Idol, CD)
1b) Am. Can. Ch. Paradym Keep Me Posted, Am. Can. CD (b) (by Am. Can. Ch. Moraine Hold That Tiger)
1c) Am. Can. Ch. Paradym Post Parade (b) (by Am. Can. Ch. Moraine Hold That Tiger)
2a) Can. Ch. Paradym What's The Latest (b) (by Am. Ch. Terrydale's Int'l Affair)
2b) Am. Can. Ch. Paradym Red Rebel (d) (by Am. Ch. Stoneridge Fairewood Flyer, CD)
2c) Can. Ch. Paradym Double Diamond (b) (by Am. Ch. Stoneridge Fairewood Flyer, CD)
2d) Can. Ch. Paradym Maudite To Premaire (b) (by Am. Ch. Stoneridge Fairewood Flyer, CD)
2e) Can. Ch. Paradym Rickard's Red (d) (by Am. Ch. Stoneridge Fairewood Flyer, CD)
2f) Can. Ch. Paradym The Printmaker (d) (by Am. Ch. Finlair Scottshire Mako)
2g) Am. Can. Ch. Paradym So Surreal (b) (by Am. Ch. Finlair Scottshire Mako)
3a) Can. Ch. Oakrun's Blue Jay Of Paradym (d) (by Am. Ch. Serendipity's Eagles Wings).

REGALRIDGE – Lee Stevens and Ken Curran
Regalridge have been breeding Airedale and Welsh Terriers since the early 1980s and have approximately 60 Champions of Record, with many dual American and Canadian Championships. In 1989, they were fortunate enough to acquire Am. Can. Ch. Tartan Texas Ranger. Ranger had been the Top Airedale in the USA two years earlier and quickly won Lee and Ken's hearts as well as adding tremendously to their breeding program. He was used extensively in the US but less frequently in Canada, other than at their kennel, but he produced many top dogs in the US as well as in Eastern Canada and one litter in Ontario. The top producing Airedale bitch to date is Ch. Regalridge Stella Attraction. With six Champions to date, including

Regalridge Piece O' The Rock, she will leave a tremendous legacy on which to build in years to come.

Am. Can. Ch. Regalridge Piece O' The Rock, or 'Darwin', is the kennel's most recent BIS winning dog, having finished his Championship in Canada and the USA, which includes Reserve Winners Dog on Montgomery Weekend two years ago. He was owner-handled to all but the Montgomery win. He is a particularly striking Airedale, with great attitude as well as type, the son of Ch. Tartan Hook 'Em Horns, (Cowboy's litter brother), and followed in his mother's footsteps with his BIS win. Ed Dickson gave Jody her best noting. It was the first time he had ever awarded an Airedale a BIS. He also won the Pictou's Centennial Show. Darwin is line-bred on Tartan Texas Ranger.

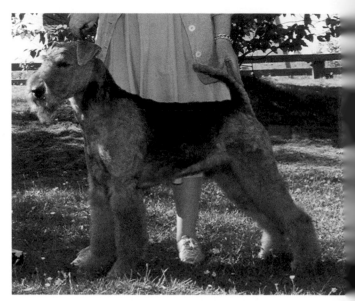

Am. Can. Ch. Regalridge Piece O' The Rock. His dam, Ch. Regalridge Stella Attraction is the top producing Airedale bitch to date.

Some of the Pedigree Breeders Awards won by Regalridge over the years are:
1991: Ch. Regalridge Western Beachrock (Ch. Cymbeline Orange Julius x Ch. Regalridge Watch A Rising Star).
Ch. Tartan Ha'Penny Of Regalridge (Am. Can. Ch. Tartan Texas Ranger x Tartan Texas Classic Star).
Ch. Regalridge Mr Beau Jangles (Ch. Tartan Southern Chieftain x Ch. Terra Nova Class Act Regalridge).
Ch. Regalridge Northern Navigator (Ch. Tartan Texas Ranger x Tartan Classic Texas Star).
Ch. Regalridge Gone With The Wind (Ch. Tartan Texas Ranger x Ch. Terra Nova Class Act Regalridge).
The following record of Champions is for the 1993 awards:
Ch. Regalridge Marshal Dillon and Ch.

Regalridge Amelia Airedale (Am. Can. Ch. Tartan Texas Ranger x Ch. Regalridge Stella Attraction).
Ch. Regalridge Word Of Caution (Am. Can. Ch. Tartan Southern Chieftain x Ch. Regalridge Steel Magnolias).
Ch. Regalridge Maritime Weste (Am. Can. Ch. Tartan Texas Ranger x Ch. Terra Nova Class Act Regalridge).
Also winning the 1994 Pedigree Breeders Award and again in 1995, the following were Champions:
Ch. Regalridge Piece O' The Rock
Ch. Regalridge Comic Opera
Ch. Regalridge's Lorna Doone
Ch. Regalridge My Time Has Come.
All the above were sired by Ch. Tartan Hook 'Em Horns and the dam was Ch. Regalridge Stella Attraction.

12 THE AIREDALE WORLDWIDE

SCANDINAVIA

FINLAND
by Pirjo Hjelm
Airedales have been steadily popular in Finland since the beginning of the century. In 1970s, 80s, and the first half of the 90s, registration numbers have been around 100-150 per year.

Tail docking became unlawful in Finland in 1996 and Airedale registrations dropped from 84 that year to 48 in 1997, rising again again to 80 in 1998. Breeders have been waiting to see how a long tail looks! Finnish Airedalers subscribe to a magazine *Karvakuona* (hairy nose), which includes new registrations. Membership of the national Airedale club is around 800-900.

In Finland, Airedales need a prize in working competition or a character-test pass before they can become Finnish Champions. They are used for tracking people and can make good search dogs. Some specialise in water rescue, a competition originally created for Newfoundlands etc. Certain owners are interested in Agility, and their Airedales love it. They can also become good Obedience dogs – a good day! Individual Airedales are currently used in hunting; a few can fetch birds from water like Retrievers.

TOP IMPORTS
Towards the beginning of the 80s certain imports had a great influence on Airedales.

Multi Ch. Big Lady's Good Gracious, bred and owned by Pirjo Hjelm.

Multi Ch. Big Lady's Bombshell, owned by Marie-Louise Molander.

Est. Int. Ch. Soft-Air Taisca, owned and bred by Ritva Josefsson.

Int. Fin. Swed. Nor. FINV-81 Ch. Tintara Bulrush (Searchlight Topscore x Eng. Ch. Tintara Upstart), breeder Pat Crome (Tintara), owner Kaisa Railo (Extempore), had some quality litters, and her offspring were especially known for good temperament and better than average hip-scores. Among Bulrush's puppies were Int. Ch. Big Lady's Xpress Xebec, born 1980, dam Fin. Ch. Big Lady's Pamela, breeder P. Hjelm, owner Jouri Tlones, and Big Lady's Yapping Yo-Ya, also born in 1980 by Int. Ch. Big Lady's Paparera, breeder/owner P. Hjelm. She was known as the dam of Int. Ch. Big Lady's Good Gracious.

Int. Ch. Baby Of Bengal came from Ruth Millar in the UK (Karudon) to Eeva Salonen (Hiuhaun). He also had some quality puppies – best known perhaps Soft-Air Erika, breeder/owner Ritva Josefsson.

Third to come to Finland was Eng. Int. Ch. FIN-80/82/83/84, NORDV-80/82/83 Mynair Nevergivin, breeder Arthur and Mavis Lodge (Mynair), owner Marie-Louise Molander von Bonsdorff, who saw the young dog in the Mynair kennels. He also had some winning offspring, among them Int. Ch. Big Lady's Adorable Child, born 1981, dam Fin. Ch. Big Lady's Tawny Tanja,

and Int. Ch. Big Lady's Good Gracious, plus litter sister Big Lady's Gin Bitter, born 1982 by BL Yapping Yo-Yo.

In 1984 Pat Crome (Tintara, UK) had a litter by Eng. Ch. Jokyl Smart Enough x Tintara Icando, and two bitches came to Finland. Fin. Dk. Ch. Tintara Much-Am-I went to Kaisa Railo (Extempore) and Int. Fin. Swed. Nor. Dk. Est. Ch., FINV-86/87/89, NORDV-86 Tintara Much-Enough to Pirjo Hjelm (Big Lady's). Both bitches became dams of several Champions all born in the Big Lady's kennel. T. Much-Am-I had puppies as follows: Fin. Est. Ch. BL X-Temperal; Fin. Ch. BL X-Clusive; Int. Ch. BL Russet Dancer, who was in turn dam of Int. Ch. EUV-94 BL Intense Dancer (WW 89, Dk. Germ. Czech. Ch. Perrancourt Pirate Prince) and grand-dam of Int. Ch. BL Bellflower, Am. It. & Int. Ch. BL Busy Body (owner Francesca Cassin, Italy) and Int. TsR. Cyp. Gr. Est. Rus. Ch. BL Businessman, owned by Ilana Moshevskaya, Israel. The latter three are sired by Int. Ch. BL Urban Cowboy.

Ch. Tintara Much-Enough or 'Nosy', had her first litter in 1988 with Swed. Ch. Jokyl Walkie Talkie, best known of which is Teija Kosola's Int. Ch. Bl Useful Enough. Nosy had a litter with

Int. Dk. Fin. Ch. EUV-91 Spicaway Ouzo, who spent 1990 in Finland with Pirjo Hjelm, becoming Top Airedale of that year and also Top Terrier 1990 in Finland. This litter produced Int. Ch. BL Doing Enough, Int. Ch. BL Deedful Enough and Int. Ch. BL Dainty Enough, the latter living in Estonia. Another daughter of Spicaway Ouzo x BL Mystic Melody (daughter of Int. Ch. BL Good Gracious) is Multi-Ch. Big Lady's Bombshell, owner Marie-Louise Molander von Bonsdorff. Bombshell had her first litter in 1994, by artificial insemination from Eng. Ch. Jokyl Lucky Strike. This litter became a real lucky strike, containing It. Ch. Big Lady's Unicorn (owner Cucca Sommi Picenardi in Italy), Swed. Ch. BL Ursa Major, Int. Ch. BL Urban Cowboy, Fin. & Est. Ch. BL Urban Vernalis and Fin. Swed. Dk. Ch. BL Ultimate in Finland. Her second litter with World Winner 1989 Multi Ch. Perrancourt Pirate Prince contained Multi Ch. BL Your Majesty, Terrier of the Year in Sweden 1998, Nor. Ch. BL Young Promise, Fin. Ch. BL Yes Please, Fin. Ch. BL Yellow Rose, and Fin. Swed. Est. Ch. BL Yet Again,

Int. Ch. BL Dainty Enough had her first litter in Finland in 1992 by WW 1989, Multi Ch. Perrancourt Pirate Prince. In this 'M' litter was Int. Ch. BL Manipulator (owner Katja Kartijarslovji, Estonia), among whose other wins was Top Dog Estonia 1996.

Ch. Big Lady's Your Majesty was Top Airedale in Sweden 1996, 1997 and 1998, and in Finland 1997 and 1998. He has multiple Group wins, was bred by Pirjo Hjelm, and is owned by Dodo Sandahl, Terttu Lardner and Svenning Jakobsen.

TOP BREEDER

Airedale breeder Pirjo Hjelm (Big Lady) was 1996 Top Breeder in Finland All Breeds. Pirjo's kennel in Jarvenpan (near Helsinki) started in 1975 with Finnish-bred Fin. Swed. Ch. Pepita whose grandsire, Invader Of Mynair, is behind most of Big Lady's dogs.

Ritva Josefsson (Soft-Air) has been breeding Airedales for more than 20 years. Puppies from her kennels have travelled to many parts of world: Estonia, Sweden, Norway, Switzerland, Portugal and Russia. She has bred many International, Scandinavian, Russian and Finnish Champions.

In 1989 Ritva imported a bitch from Berit Forsman of the UK's Beacytan Kennels, Ch. Hilane High Society Of Beacytan. This bitch went on to be the best Airedale terrier in Finland 1991, Europe 1991, and World '91. Her

Fin. Ch. Soft-Air Xyster, bred by Ritva Josefsson, owned by Tarjm Laustela.

puppies, Soft-Air Taisca and SA Top Knot, have been extremely successful. Another of her dogs, Soft-Air Must Be Funny, was Top Obedience Airedale 1991, 1992, and 1993.

In 1992 Ritva Josefsson received a Finnish Kennel Club award for distinguished breeding work.

SWEDEN

The situation for Swedish Airedalers has changed dramatically in the last ten years since a docking ban came into effect in 1989. Registrations have halved to around 100 dogs at the present time.

The 1980s ended with two bitches at the top. These were Ch. Pinto Rum And Coca Cola, owned and bred by Pia Lundberg and Ruth Rudenholt, and Ch. Soft-Air Living Eyes, bred in Finland by Ritva Josefsson and owned by Ulla Fagerlund, of kennel Ferryman.

Multi Ch. Big Lady's Your Majesty, bred by Pirjo Hjelm, owned by Sandahl, Lardner and Jakobsen.

In the autumn of 1989 the two-year-old Ch. Jokyl Special Delivery was imported by Borje and Monica Gustavson (RiverAire), Gunilla Pastarus (Tiggus) and Dodo Sandahl (Sandale). Special Delivery was Top Airedale in 1990, 1991 and 1992. He managed to win BIS at ten Airedale Specialties, the last two from Veteran class, and was also a Group winner. A successful show dog, he also left his mark as a stud, being the sire of many Champions.

Stig Ahlberg imported an interesting dog from the UK's Ken Ventress (Junken). Ch. Junaken Vulton, a Group winner, demonstrated his abilities as a sire through many champions, not least out of Pinto bitches. One of these, Ch. Pinto Wish Upon A Star, wrote history by being exported to Australia in whelp to Ch. Malmongen Stranger In Paradise. In 1992 two of her puppies, by the famous American dog Ch. MJ's Stone Ridge Chosen One, were brought to Sweden by the Pinto kennels. The dog, who was to be Ch. Yorkpark Pinto Ringo Star, is owned by Sonija Johansson (Malmangen). The fresh bloodline was interesting to many breeders and Ringo Star was used with very good results. The Australian bitch puppy was to become Ch. Yorkpark Pinto Star On Ice. She stayed with the Pinto kennel and has become the proud dam of many Champions.

Karin Dahlberg (Karmadale), in the north of Sweden, made two Australian imports: Ch. Tjurings Inxs who became a Group winner and sire to several Champions, and the bitch Ch. Tjuringa Krest. The home-bred Ch. Karmadale's Kibowi Cocktail, also a Group winner, kept the Airedale flag flying in northern Sweden. The equally successful

Swed. Ch. Tiggus Special Combination (undocked).

littermates, Ch. Ferrymans Beautiful Eyes and Ch. Ferrymans Dark Eyes, by the German import Ch. Hugo v.d. Shonenberg ex Ch. Soft-Air Living Eyes, kept the breed in the limelight in the south of Sweden.

In the early 1990s, the Pinto kennels had great success, especially at Malmo in 1991.

The first, and in 1998 still the only, undocked Airedale to be the top-winner in the breed, appeared in 1993. Ch. Tiggus Special Combination, bred by Gunilla Pastarus and co-owned by Dodo Sandahl, took over the title of Top Airedale from her sire Special Delivery.

Int. Ch. Pinto Rum And Coca Cola made a comeback as a Veteran in 1994 when she was Top Airedale. During that year, borders with other west European countries were opened to show dogs, who can now visit many countries but not without extensive inoculations and paperwork. Sweden is visited by foreign exhibitors, such as Pirjo Hjelm (Big Lady's, Finland), a frequent visitor who has taken many Champion titles back home. In 1994, Am. Ch. Darbywoods

Preferred Stock, owned by Rita Ahle in Denmark, was used successfully by many Swedish breeders.

In 1994 and 1995 more imports were made. Stig Ahlberg (Ragtime) brought in Ch. Stargus Shooting Times Of Saredon, a younger full-brother to the well-known UK Ch. Stargus War Lord. Terttu Lardner had two dogs out of the remarkable brood-bitch Ch. Big Lady's Bombshell, namely Ch. Big Lady's Ursa Major (AI by Ch. Jokyl Lucky Strike) and Ch. Big Lady's Your Majesty (by Ch. Perrancourt Pirate Prince) in Czechoslovakia. The latter was co-owned by Svenning Jakobsen and Dodo Sandahl. Ch. Copperstone Requisition won in Sofiero and was top winning Airedale male in 1995. He was just beaten for the top spot by Dodo Sandahl's import Ch. Jokyl Extravaganza, another Group winner.

In 1996, two new Group winning dogs emerged: Ch. Pinto Sound Of Silence, owned by Lotta Walles, and Ch. Pinto After All, owned by Hanna Hedendal. The latter also won BIS at the Airedale Terrier Guild's 30th anniversary show.

Group winner in 1997 was Ch. Copperstone Melody Polka (by the aforementioned Copperstone Requisition), owned and bred by Maureen Klerell.

The new big winner of the period was Ch. Big Lady's Your Majesty. He was Top Airedale in Sweden 1996, '97 and '98, and in Finland 1997 and '98. He has many Group placings in Sweden, Denmark and Finland and won BIS two days in a row when Voormland-Dals Terrier Club celebrated 20 years in 1998. The same year he had a fantastic run of wins to take him to the Top Terrier title.

It is the first time since 1981, when Ch. Ragtime Sassafras was the winner, that an Airedale won Top Terrier in Sweden.

It was also a good year for his young daughter Sandale Cover Girl (out of Jokyl Extravaganza), owned and bred by Dodo Sandahl. She won the grand title of Junior World Winner at the World Show in Finland, undocked and under an American judge. She also won a Group and was the top winning bitch in 1998, but is not yet a Champion, since in Sweden you have to win the last certificate when the dog is over two years old.

Active breeders other than the ones mentioned above are Gunnel Lindberg and Susanne Sparre (Coastguard), Tina Wallin (Spiceyard), Agneta Groning, (Lydiaire), Kerstin Elfner (Airedynamic), Mia Lindberg (Knosos), Ann-Marie Figved (Mio Monello), Anita and Ake Magnusson (Fair Trial's), Kerstin and Sten Olsson (Jackeroo's), Lotta Streiffert (Lovestorm's), Pia Wahstrom (Aerobic's), among others.

DENMARK

The Spicaway kennels are known worldwide. Int. Dk. Fin. Ch. EUV-91 Ch. Spicaway Ouzo (Ch. Perrancourt Pirate x Jokyl Fancy Dandy) had the best of bloodlines. He was Club winner 1988 and Top Airedale 1989 for breeders/owners Inge Hansen and Mikael Laursen. He spent 1990 in Finland with Pirjo Hjelm, becoming Top Airedale of that year and also Top Terrier. Ouzo has sired many Champions throughout Europe. Inge and Mikael imported one of my favourite dogs, Eng. Ch. Shadli Likely Lad, bred by Al and Jan Favell. He was a gentleman, with a super character.

RUSSIA

Airedale Terriers were the first breed of terriers to appear in Russia. At the beginning of the Russo-Japanese war in 1904, the Russian embassy in London approached Lt. Col. Richardson, the recognised authority in the field of military dog-breeding at the time, with a request to help provide the Russian army with dogs specially trained to take the wounded away from the battlefields. Richardson promptly responded, and, in due course, his terriers were sent to St Petersburg, the Russian capital at the time. Most of these dogs were Airedales which were soon accepted by the Russian army as the best dogs for communication and sanitary services. These Airedales had been imported from England.

The Airedale in Russia had mixed fortunes until the 1980s when it became well established.

Rus. Ch. New Spring Fancy Modern Type, bred by N. Kirsanjva and M. Hohlova, owned by G. Rudenkova.

Rus. Ch. Strongfort Podarok, bred by G. Lesh, owned by N. Kirsanova.

Both the original Airedale Terriers and their masters/breeders perished in the Bolshevik revolution of October 1917. Airedales were reintroduced in Russia in the early 1920s when the breed was recognised as useful for defence departments.

Special Red Army units of service dogs were created in 1923, and Airedales were also used successfully as demolition dogs, guard dogs, police tracking dogs and casualty dogs. Russia brought dozens of Airedales through official channels from Britain and Germany, and began target-breeding of Airedales. As a result, this breed grew in numbers and popularity.

After World War II, Russia had to restore the breed from two sources: a handful of Airedales remaining in Moscow and those just brought in from Germany, some of them captured during the war. Until 1959, Russian breeders relied too heavily on inbreeding, which brought forth accumulated genetic defects and resulted in loss of a distinct breed type.

In the 1960s, international contacts first became possible for Russian dog breeders. Several dogs were brought to Russia from East Germany and Czechoslovakia. All the new Airedales had close genealogical links with Europe. They originated from key sires in the breed, such as Warland Protector of Sheltrock, Brineland Bonnie Boy, Clie Courtier and Warland Ditto, some of the greatest sires of the 1920s.

By the mid-1980s, the Airedale breed was well established in Russia and was immensely popular. The Czech Airedales, tracing their origin from Din First Fire and through the line of his son Bumbarash, constituted the majority of the Moscow Airedale community.

In fact, the situation with Russia's Airedales was not quite as good as it

Rus. Ch. Spicaway Brutus (Denmark).

seemed. Foreign contact was very limited and Russian Airedales were effectively sealed off from the rest of the world, getting an occasional injection of fresh blood from East Germany or Czechoslovakia. These infrequently imported dogs were certainly not up to a high standard. There was little or no information about winners of major international shows; few dog yearbooks or catalogues of dog photographs were available. Yet the Russian judges were popularly considered competent Airedale experts overseas.

Domestic breeders followed a set of homespun standards approved by the Ministry for Agriculture rather than the internationally accepted FCI (Fédération Cynologique Internationale) standards. The Russian Breed Standard required a greater height, with subsequent changes in shape and proportions. Lack of information on Airedales and absence of reliable benchmarks prevented domestic breeders from identifying and correcting a number of deviations and defects. Domestic Airedales tended to follow very old standards, long-since abandoned elsewhere.

In the early 1980s, five pedigree Airedales recently descended from English truebloods came from Finland (four) and France (one). They helped update the Russian breed of Airedale and made them look more like their cousins overseas. Their names were Teinikedon Ulimus (a prize-winner, later dubbed 'Tobik', who made an especially great impact on the breed in Russia; owner S. Smolanitskaya); males Scherzo De Franc Sablon, Big Lady's All Attention, and bitches Echo-Lotta (owner Ms Larshina), and Big Lady's Covergirl Elisa. The grandsire of Scherzo De Franc Sablon and Echo-Lotta was Jokyl Smart Guy, an excellent Airedale. Other dogs hailed from the leading Finnish kennels with excellent Scandinavian lineage. Swed. Fin. Nor. Ch. Bengal Mogul was grandsire to Big Lady's Covergirl Elisa and great-grandsire to Big Lady's All Attention through his son Royal Tan Roderick, also a Champion of Sweden and Norway. Through his other son, Boogeyman, he was grandsire of Teinikedon Ulimus. Another popular Finnish Airedale was in Tobik's pedigree – Malmangen Goldpowder, tracing his origin to dogs raised in the best known English kennels, Krescent, Bengal and Siccawei.

These bloods soon improved the quality of the breed and the Russian Airedale became more modern and elegant and more like proper terriers.

Tobik's participation in breeding was particularly valuable. In appearance, he was materially different from other Russian Airedale Terriers at that time, even from locally acknowledged best specimens. He had strong genes, passing his best qualities on to his offspring: a beautiful head, a great body, a good coat of hair, etc. Teinikedon Ulimus was the first Russian Airedale Terrier to produce descendants of such quality and uniformity. The Ulimus children and grandchildren won at dog shows wherever Finnish blood was added to Airedales. Matings of Tobik with Finnish bitches also produced some outstanding results, as his blood was mixed with that of Scherzo De Frank Sablon.

By the 1980s, Moscow and Leningrad were no longer Russia's only centres breeding Airedales. Large Airedale sections were organised in Saratov, Rostov, Minsk, Vladimir, Ekaterinburg and Perm.

Dogs from Saratov often won top places at major dog shows. Saratov's breeders widely used Teinikedon Ulimus, in-breeding on him 2-2 (where Tobik was the grandsire on both mother's and father's sides). Their competent breeding soon produced good results; Saratov dogs from the Style club led at the largest shows in the country. Echo-Lotta's offspring from Rostov-on-Don were an important factor in successful breeding of Airedales in Saratov. Echo-Lotta produced a large progeny, including bitches Pifaldina Pride (owner Kostyuk), Duchess Pride (owner Kuropatkina), and Pifaldina's daughters, Michaela Style (owner Yerokhina) and Minion Style (owner Kvasha). Michaela and Minion's litter-sisters Marjolene Style (owner Kanniniex, Riga), Marilyn Style (owner Pryzhukova, Odessa), and Musetta Style (Rostov-on-Don) won at the dog shows in their respective cities. They had many litters and gave birth to large families.

Tobik's lineage was further developed in Moscow-based clubs – MGOLS (Russian abbreviation for Moscow City

Rus. Ch. Quick Fly Tinkler, owned by Elizarova and Terhouich.

Society of Dog Enthusiasts; Chairperson for Airedale Division N. Kirsanova) and Elite (Head Breeder S. Smolanitskaya). Dogs raised and trained in these clubs won at many dog shows. The winners include Hunter Pride (owner Ms Rubina), Negoro Ergunt (owner Mr Terentiev), Lisbeth Pride (owner N. Kirsanova), Tornado Twist (owner Ms Budnik), Trassy Twist (owner M. Khokhlova), and many more.

Perestroika of the late 1980s brought a crisis upon Russian dog-breeding which soon began to take its toll on Airedale Terriers. Before then, most Airedales had been concentrated in official DOSAAF dog clubs, of which the DOSAAF club in Moscow was the largest and best-equipped. Moscow held two city shows every year, plus two regional shows, which attracted many participants, with some of the finest specimens of the breed in Russia. This made the title of a Moscow show winner very prestigious. The dogs exhibited at Moscow shows reflected the actual state of affairs in the breed; these shows registered successes and failures of breeding. Between 50 and

Rus. Ch. Rollingstones To Russia With Love (centre) with his progeny at the national club's show.

60 dogs in each age group took part in the shows from 1985 to 88.

Between 1987 and 1989, dog associations and clubs sprouted everywhere across Russia; the breed became split into sub-breeds. People involved in Airedale breeding were not always competent, and changes and divisions in the breed were not always for the better. Moreover, the names of Teinikedon Ulimus, Scherzo and Echo-Lotta were becoming ever more distant in the family trees, and the effect of English blood was waning.

Recent political change meant that Russian breeders could now cross borders at will and see European Airedales. Foreign literature about the breed became more available, as well as providing more reliable comparisons. It became clear that our 'Finns' did not possess some of the very important features of a modern Airedale's appearance.

From the late 1980s to date, more than 40 Airedale dogs and 20 bitches were brought to the USSR (and later NIS) from 12 countries around the world. Few other breeds in Russia can boast of such extensive imports.

The first imported dogs opened a new page in history of the breed in Russia; it was not merely a transition to new dogs with different lineage, to a new vision of the Airedale breed, to new organisation of breeding, to stricter criteria for selection and breeding. Thus Russia joined the civilised dog world.

New private and co-operative kennels replaced the centralised authoritarian dog clubs where often-misguided staff 'zootechnicians' would arbitrarily impose a set of breed criteria. The new private kennels specialise exclusively in Airedales, gathering dogs with the most interesting exterior, which represent valuable breed material. Stiff competition has propelled several Airedale kennels into eminence: Style (Saratov, head breeders Alla Yerokhina, Galina Kuropatkina,) Bright

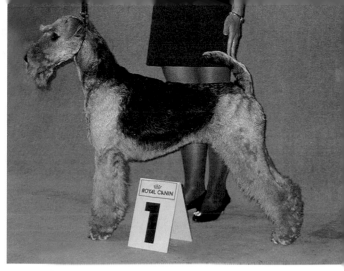

Nose (Moscow, breeder Elena Lapina), Catherina's (Tallinn, breeder Ekaterina Kantievskaya), Stunning (Ekaterinburg, breeder Natalya Stafeyeva), Cornels (Moscow, Elena and Sergey Nikulina), Basidale (Saratov, breeder Vasili Turin), Modern Type (Moscow, breeder Natalya Kirsanova), Excellent (Moscow, breeder Nina Chichkova), Quick Fly (Moscow, breeders Elizaveta and Irina Elizarov), Gypsy (Moscow, breeder Inna Danilova). Local clubs, private kennels and breeders unite into National Airedale Clubs.

The winners display careful trimming and training. Presentation of dogs at shows is becoming increasingly important. It is often hard to say (even for a casually observing expert) how much in the winner comes from nature, and how much from hard training, trimming and handling by the ambitious master. Even foreign experts note that the beauty of Russian Airedales is now on a par with the best Airedales overseas.

Though modern Russian Airedales have totally different origins, the current success is not totally isolated from

Rus. Ch. Cornels Great Beauty, owned by E. & S. Nikulina and S. Lebedeva.

previous achievements. 'Old' Airedales made the breed well known and much loved in Russia. Dedicated Airedale enthusiasts have accumulated a wealth of experience over the years: Natalya Kirsanova, Emily Nogachevskaya, Sergei and Elena Nikulina, Elisaveta and Irina Elizarov, Julia Lakatosh, Ekaterina Senashenko, Anna Stouit (Moscow), Galina Kuropatkina and Alla Yerokhina (Saratov), Marina Bezukladova (St Petersburg), and Natalia Stafeyeva (Ekaterinburg), among others, have devoted more than fifteen years of their lives to Airedales.

Russian breed material now includes some of the best modern blood in the breed. Airedales have become serious competition to other breeds in Best in Group and Best in Show inter-breed contests. Nobody is really surprised any longer that our Airedales win such contests. Strongfort Xterminator, Basidale Sea Rover Of Constanta, Kornels Great Beauty, Kron Berry, It's My Life Kornels, Spicaway Brutus have all won in the Terrier class; others are poised to win in the near future.

Some Russian dogs have participated in foreign shows, and won top places and awards. Soft-Air Vichy, Britham

Rus. Ch. Danish Queen Cornels, owned by E. & S. Nikulina.

Pendragon Wrath-Amon, Epoch International Time, are all Finnish Champions.

Eight Russian male Airedales and ten bitches took part in the 1998 World Show in Helsinki, and were described as excellent by the jury. Five dogs and six bitches won prizes: Quick Fly Temptation (Rollingstones To Russia With Love x Rotbi Darfly Bright), owned by Lisa Elisarova, won Res. CACIB. All this gives us hope that Airedales, this favourite breed, has a great future, and that new, more numerous Airedale generations will be capable of winning at the world's most prestigious shows.

ESTONIA

Airedales in Estonia have long been popular due to Russian heritage. Estonian Airedale breeders became interested in western lines in the 1980s, their previous lines coming from Russia, Czechoslovakia and East Germany. The first Western Airedale to arrive in Estonia from Finland in 1989 was Big Lady's K-Temoral (Int. Ch. Tintara Bulrush x Fin. Dk. Ch. Tintara Much-Am-I), later to become Fin. Est. Champion. Her owner is Katja Kantijevslaja (Katherina's Land), who later imported a Finnish bitch, Red Diadem's Barbie (Ragtime King Oliver x Red Diadem's Afrodite). The first litter was Katherina's A-litter – Est. Ch. Katherina's Active Baby became a Group winner and her brother Rus. Ch. Katherina's Amorow Gambler is famous in Russia. Katja's big dream was to get a bitch puppy from Int. Ch. Tintara Much-Enough, and in 1990 her dream came true. Big Lady's Dainty Enough (later to become Int. Fin. Est. Dk. Lux. Ch. and Junior World Winner 91) arrived as an import from Finland.

This bitch's first litter was born in Finland – Big Lady's 1992 M-litter, sire Multi-Ch. World Winner 1989 Perrancourt Pirate Prince. Katja chose a

Int. Ch. Katherina's Land Happy Estonia.

Multi Ch. Big Lady's Manipulator: Top Dog Estonia All Breeds 1996.

dog puppy – Big Lady's Manipulator –
who became the biggest winning
Airedale in Estonia ever, Top Dog All
Breeds 1996 (after winning second place
the year before).

A 1996 litter (Int. Ch. Big Lady's
Urban Cowboy x Est. Ch. Katherina's
Land Canary Sarah) has produced a few
young winners.

Katherina's Land Hot Rock quickly
became Int. Ch., also winning Groups. A
litter sister owned by Pirjo Hjelm, Fin.
Swed. Int. Ch. Katherina's Land Happy,
has been shown with good results.

Estonia also has some imports from
the famous Spicaway kennels in
Denmark and some Soft-Air in Finland.

IRELAND
by Roy Gregg

Two of Ireland's leading Airedale kennels
are Bambusa and Mynight.

In 1979, Roy and Marion Gregg of
Bambusa used Ch. Siccawei Galliard,
then at stud in the Jokyl kennel, a mating
which produced three Irish champions,
Bambusa Noble Lord, Byzantium and
Grecian Urn. For three years, 1980-82,
these dogs dominated Airedales in
Ireland, but missed out on Group wins
at Championship show level.

The Greggs bought Purston Treble
Chance and Sueman Cintroid from
Michael Collings (Purston). Before being
exported in 1981, Noble Lord served
Sueman Cintroid and the litter produced
Ir. Ch. Bambusa Cherubim (1980),
Bambusa's first Group and BIS winner at
Championship show level. Byzantium
was retired from the show ring and taken
to Ch. Jokyl Smart Enough and the
product, Ir. Ch. Bambusa Camelot
(1984), won several Groups and BIS.

*Ir. Eng. Ch. Bambusa Gentry, bred and
owned by Roy and Marion Gregg.*

Purston Treble Chance contributed via
his son, Ir. Ch. Bambusa Montage
(1985), who retired with an injury one
week after winning BIS. During his two-
year career, Monty won every puppy and
junior class in which he competed and
helped continue the line through his son
Ir. Ch. Bambusa Scholar (1988), winner
of four Groups and one BIS.

Camelot's son, Bambusa Blackthorn,
having won a Terrier Group and Reserve
BIS, was retired early to make way for
the kennel's most notable show dog, UK
& Ir. Ch. Bambusa Gentry (1990), sired
by Ir. Ch. Bambusa Scholar. Gentry is
the only Irish-bred Airedale ever to have
gained his English title. In 1991, he was
Top Airedale Puppy in the UK. In 1992,
aged 18 months he won the Terrier
Group at the Irish KC St Patrick's Day
Show. Gentry set all manner of records
and was always placed one to four in the
Group at over 20 shows – truly a quality
dog. Another Camelot pup became Ir.
Ch. Bambusa Lancelot (1992).

A bitch mated to the Huxleys' Ch.
Robroyd Jet produced Ir. Ch. Bambusa
Tapestry (1995), first shown in 1996,
aged nine months. Tapestry won BoB
and Group four. She was not shown
seriously again until, at a selection of

Open and Championship shows from 98-99, she won seven Groups, a Res.BIS and two BIS. From Ch. Robroyd Jet's line comes the nine-months-old Bambusa Sugar & Spice (1998), winner of Puppy Stakes and reserve Green Star. She will be mated to a dog from Judy Averis, Saredon Neon Light At Bambusa, who has just won BoB at the age of twelve months.

At Mynight, Sean and Eileen Knight's first Airedale was Mynair Manabout (Swed. Ch. Copperstone Hannibal Hayes x Mynair I'm It), from breeders Arthur and Mavis Lodge (Mynair). His first IKC show on St Patrick's Day 1982 brought them BoB under German Airedale specialist Rudi Tegeler. When Manabout was shown in veterans, he won a total of 61 Best Veteran prizes between Champion stakes and Open shows. Another Mynair, Mr Gracious (Hector), went on to become a Champion and went BoB at the IKC Championship show, under judge Mrs Margaret Hanson (USA). The next bitch was Mynair Love & Laughter, or 'Amy' (Dendaric Glen Grant x Mynair Fairy Queen), who gained her Championship title and became Annual Champion – Top Airedale in the breed in 1991 and produced three litters. Jonvias Beach Comber (Eng. Ch. Jokyl Lucky Strike x Eng. Ch. Dendaric Hot Stuff), known as Flint, went to Bambusa in 1992 from John and Sylvia Hicks (Jonvias). He has won numerous Best Puppy awards and has won at the IKC Ch. Show under judges Mrs P. Heikkinen (Fin), H.E. Gruttener (Ger), Mr X.A. Hekl (Switzerland) and Mr R. Chasoudian (USA); in 1996 BoB (no CACIB); 1997-8 winning CACIB with BoB; 1999 Res. BoB with CACIB; three Terrier Group 1;

two Group 2, Res. BIS. Flint gained his Championship title in 1996 and became Annual Champion in 1996 (Top Airedale) and again in 1998, also winning the BoB at the Airedale Terrier Club Ireland Championship Show in August 1998. To date he has won a total of 45 BoBs, a record to be proud of.

Ir. Ch. Mynight Molly (Ir. Ch. Jonvias Beach Comber x Ir. Ch. Mynair Love & Laughter) has won a lot during her show career and was Res. CACIB at IKC Ch. Show 1997. Molly has produced Ir. Ch. Mynight Happy Memory ('Trudy'), sired by Eng. Ch. Robroyd Granite. Trudy was overall Top Winning Bitch in the Breed for 1998.

GERMANY
by Rudi Tegeler

A top English sire, Brineland Bonnie Boy, won both of the first shows in Germany after World War II, but was stopped thereafter by Rural Wyrewood Apollo. Bonnie Boy's owner sold him to a Belgian breeder, Louis Petit, who died in 1948, and Herr Burgmer of the Artmann kennel in Wuppertal bought the dog which he had already used at stud. Burgmer was one of the first German breeders to visit English shows after the war. He knew about the successes Miss Jones scored with her Burdale kennel, built up with Brineland Bonnie Boy's son, Lineside Marquis.

Top German breeder Rudi Tegeler (Vom Kirm) acquired a dog puppy from a Bonnie Boy father x daughter mating and still maintains this line which he contends, has influenced significantly the breeding of Airedales on the continent.

Vom Kirm's success started with the dog Ch. Etzel vom Kirm, a son of

168

Artmanns Moritz. His sire was Brineland Bonnie Boy. With both sires and staying very close to the line, Tegeler has bred continuous winners, including Othello vom Kirm who became Eng. Ch. under the name of Jokyl Othello. Othello's dam was Hera vom Kirm and the sire, Edzel vom Kirm, was her half-brother. The sire of both the dogs was a son of Brineland Bonnie Boy, Artmanns Moritz. Hera's grandsire from the mother's side was Artmanns Roger, also a son of Brineland Bonnie Boy. Since 1956, Rudi has visited Crufts every year to keep in contact with successful English breeders such as Fred Cross, Mollie Harmsworth, Dorothy Hodgkinson and Bert Southgate, who worked at the Jokyl kennels.

Rudi acquired Eng. Ch. Jokyl Bengal Figaro, who had been sold to Walt Disney in order to be used in a film. Once the film was finished, the dog went to the Vom Kirm kennel. Within 18 months he became German, Dutch, Luxembourg and Int. Ch., before returning to America where he became Am. and Can. Champion. At the age of six he went back to England and won at Crufts that year.

Out of Figaro and Penny vom Kirm, Rudi bred the Champion bitch Vera vom Kirm', who later whelped World Champion Gustav Kirm vom Lohfeuer. The sire of Gustav vom Lohfeuer was Ch. Illo vom Kloster Liebenau, whose sire was Puck vom Kirm. His mother was Jenney vom Walttrautenschlosschen (whose sire was Ch. Bengal Brave, also sire of Jokyl Bengal Figaro), a perfect bitch in anatomy but with completely weak coat. Puck passed on good hair dominantly.

Eng. Ch. Kresent Bengal Brave is a son of Kresent Model Maid who produced Champions in every single litter. The sire of Model Maid was Ch. Barton of Burdale whose sire was Brineland Bonnie Boy's son, Lineside Marquis. Comparatively good bitches were whelped out of the combination of Jokyl Bengal Figaro and Jokyl Othello vom Kirm's daughter Jokyl Hera – the bitch Ch. Jokyl Elegance and one of the most beautiful Airedale bitches, Jokyl Smartie Pants, mother of the well-known dog Jokyl Gallipants.

Rudi Tegeler never abandoned his breeding line and other breeders who were prepared to try it have had success, a prominent example being the Dutch kennel 'of Malton'.

NETHERLANDS
by Martin and Roely Bouma

Malton is the name of a small Yorkshire village which has given its name to the Airedale Terrier kennel of the Bouma family in Holland. Roely Bouma's parents had bred a few litters under the name Noorderster and, when she and her husband started to take an active part in showing dogs, they came into contact with Rudi Tegeler, at that time a renowned breeder and judge of Airedale Terriers. He provided them with Holde vom Kirm, a bitch of the utmost importance to the 'Of Malton' kennels, and gave crucial help and advice on type, anatomy, trimming and breeding. Holde vom Kirm gained the Dutch Championship and has been followed by many 'of Malton' Champions.

To date, Roely and her son Martin have Champions titled as follows: 28 Dutch, 14 International, 15 German, 12 Luxembourg, three Belgian, five Austrian, six Youth World Champions, four European and three World Champions.

Multi Ch. Norma Jean Of Malton (left) and Vincente c. vom St Laurentius.

Eng. Multi Ch. Ballintober Gold Of Saredon: Winner of 32 CCs on the Continent.

The Boumas take all possible precautions to ensure that their breeding stock is free from HD (hip dysplasia). Their kennels also obtain good results in working dogs; two sisters from one litter are now in used as guide dogs.

One of Roely and Martin's major winners is Dutch. Int. World Ch. Elysa Of Malton, who became World Champion in Valencia. For BoB, she was very often in tight competition with Eng. Ch. Ballintober Gold Of Saredon. Elysa was not only a great show dog with super temperament, but also a good brood bitch. Her first litter sired by Othello vom Kirm was born in May 1993 and, from the six she whelped, four are in the show ring and are successfully winning. The two puppies the Boumas kept are Royal Dutch Of Malton, winner of many international titles, Youth World and European Champion, and his litter sister, Rose-Marie Of Malton, a smaller bitch particularly liked by the English specialists. In a European Championship in Luxembourg she won BoB under judge Barbara Holland (Tanworth), and did the same in a World Championship under Berenice Howell (Cortella). Mr Marshall made her BIS in Germany.

Pandora Of Malton (Pollux II v.d. Schonen Bergen x Holde v. Kirm) was one of the most successful European Airedales ever, winning many International shows with up to 80 entries and winning BoB many times.

BELGIUM
by Francois Graulus

Francois and Gerda Graulus (van't Asbroek) started in Airedales in 1978. Dutch bitch Lady Kim Pretender is the mother of their most successful dogs.

Pictured (Left to right): Muli Ch. Sundance van't Asbroek, Multi Ch. Victory van't Asbroek, and Uncurbed van't Asbroek.

Kim was born in 1986, a descendant of a German/English combination (Cocas Cosmos x Triple Sec of The Burg Ludwigstein). In 1991 Kim obtained the title of International Champion and in 1988 was bred to Pollux II v.d. Schonen Bergen. From this combination came Miss Melody van't Asbroek and Mister Murphy van't Asbroek, both of whom achieved the title of Multi-Champion. Miss Melody became World Winner with BoB in 1991 in Dortmund, Germany. The same mating was repeated the following year, producing Nobody van't Asbroek, owned by Brone Johan. Nobody became Multi-Champion and, in 1995, World Winner with BoB in Brussels, Belgium. His sister, Nanouska van't Asbroek, went to the Oakrun Kennels in Ontario (Canada), where she became Champion in 1991.

The kennel's successes in recent years have included.
Multi Ch. & European Winner 1997, Ch. Sexy Girl van't Asbroek
Multi Ch. & European Winner 1997, World W Helsinki 1998, Ch. Sundance van't Asbroek
Finn. Swed. Dan. Ch. Undercover van't Asbroek
European Junior Winner 1997, BIS Dutch Clubmatch 1997, Urigo van't Asbroek
Swed. Ch. Treasure van't Asbroek
BoB Paris 1998, Uncurbed van't Asbroek
BoB Norway 1998, Unique van't Asbroek
Belgian Winner 1998, Victory van't Asbroek.

FRANCE
by Fred Devitt

In France there is only one official breed club for Airedales, the various regional clubs being all-breed clubs. The Club Francais de l'Airedale Terrier et des Divers Terriers (CFAT et DT) is responsible not only for Airedales but also for all terriers in the FCI Group 3 with the exception of the two Fox Terrier breeds, the five Scottish breeds, the German Jagdterrier and the Yorkshire Terrier. Of the breeds covered by the CFAT, Airedales are the most numerous followed by the American Staffordshire Terrier. The CFAT organises one breed club championship show per year and four regional non-championship shows. At these shows the dogs are tested for their character and must pass the TAN (Test d'Aptitude Naturelle) test in order to become French champion. Winning the CACS at the breed club show or the Paris show is also a must for the title of French Champion.

171

Fr. Ch. Goofy de Catextol,
owned by Fred Devitt.

Undoubtedly the top breeder over the past thirty years was the late Alben (Gino) Isaert. He worked closely with the late Jean Campbell and imported several top Loudwells as stock for his own kennel "de Ginojack". The import, Loudwell Crown Oak, won BoB at the Paris show four times running, which must be a record for any breed.

The most consistent affix over the past ten years has been Maryse Delaye's 'du Haillet des Coneiredes'. Her use of Jokyl-based stock in the very early days and then the introduction of German stock has brought good results, as can be seen from their consistent placings at the Paris and the breed club shows.

On a smaller scale, Dominique Lepage's affix 'de Catextol' has had a lot of success, with two Champions in her first two litters and her selection several times as top breeder in the Pedigree PAL ratings. In these ratings Fred Devitt's Ch. Goofy de Catextol (Adhemar de Tanworth x Djoyce des Francs Sablons) and Maryse Delaye's Ch. Hop du Haillet des Corneiredes were joint top Airedales in 1994. Goofy's half-sister, Ch. International Love Affair de Catextol (Ch. Ballintober Gold of Saredon x Djoyce des Francs Sablons) went on to win top Airedale in 1995.

In 1996 and 1997 Jean-Marc Rossi's imported Ch. Jokyl Xmas Cracker (Ch. Jokyl Just As Smart x Ginger Dream Time At Jokyl) took the top place and, over the past three years, has had quite a spectacular career in France.

In 1996, Jokyl imports, Monique Saucet's Jokyl Xmas Wish, her litter brother Jean-Marc Rossi's Ch. Jokyl Xmas Cracker and Marc Gacon's Jokyl Diplomat scored enough points in the PAL ratings to make the Jokyl the top affix in France at the European and World Championship shows. Delaye's Ch. Hop du Haillet de Corneiredes took third place in the World Show in 1994 and second place in the Champion class in the Brussels World Show in 1995. At the 1995 European Championship Show in Luxembourg, Ch. Jokyl Xmas Cracker won his European Junior Champion title.

ITALY
by Guilio A. di Somma

The Airedale scene in Italy has remained fairly static for the last decade. The number of registrations to the LOI (Book of Origins) of the Italian Kennel Club (ENCI), which includes both home-bred and imported dogs has been steady at about 180 yearly.

Top Italian Airedale enthusiasts are, in

alphabetical order: Giulio Audisio di Somma (Iulius), Marco Galli (Lisander), Luisa Romanini (Ashgrove), Lorena Merati and Raimondo Gilardoni de' Montalto (Samarcanda), and Alessandra Sommi Picenardi (Ginger), the latter being one of the 'old guard' still exhibiting and breeding.

At the end of the 1980s two important Shadli males arrived: Shadli Lord Luke (Ginger Voila Of Stanstead x Shadli Bellona), owned by Matteucci, and Shadli Manipulator At Jokyl, known as 'Nip' (Ch. Jokyl Gallipants x Shadli Bellona), owned by Giulio Audisio and the only son of Gallipants imported into Italy. Nip has been very important both in the show ring and for reproduction. Audisio then imported an important bitch, Jokyl Spring Song, litter sister to Ch. Jokyl Lucky Strike. He chose a new stud, Stanstead Endeavour, son of Ch. Jokyl Lucky Strike, who, along with Robroyd Jet, owned by Marco Galli, has been dominant in producing good-quality offspring. Because of the extremely high quality of these two bloodlines in the 1990s, the Iulius

Airedales have constantly been of first-rate quality.

Marco Galli (Lisander Airedales) has concentrated on importing show dogs rather than producing puppies. Two studs at his kennels have, however, been important: Ital. Int. SIT Ch. Robroyd Flint at Lisander (Shadli Magnum x Robroyd Bronzite) and Ital. Eng. Int. SIT Ch. Robroyd Jet (Ch. Robroyd Granite x Ch. Robroyd Emerald Pride At Tiggis) are both Group winners and have contributed to the quality of the breed in Italy and in Europe.

Luisa Romanini (Ashgrove), wife of Roberto, the famous terrier handler, has on the other hand always looked towards the USA, importing Blackjack dogs. Her stud Blackjack Monty of Ashgrove (sire King Of The Hill) has been important; even more so is her highly-bred foundation bitch, Ch. Blackjack's Rising Star or 'Libby' (sire Blackjacks Mighty Samson). She took her title easily and retired with a BIS at SIT Special Terrier Show in Napoli 1993 under judge Axel Morke.

Libby's daughter, Ch. Morgan Le Fey (Ginevra) soon became a champion. Her last litter was sired by Eng. Ital. Ch. Robroyd Jet. Many of her puppies did well in conformation shows and Libby is now 'Campione Riproduttore'. Blackjack's Monty Of Ashgrove, imported in 1995, has just finished his Championship and was Res. CACIB in the European show this year. Ch. Blackjack's El Nino was campaigned by Ashgrove in 1999, becoming an Italian Champion, and the kennel is proud to be one of the first Airedale breeders in Italy doing official hip scores on breeding stock.

Samarcanda have imported from

It. Int. Ch. Stanstead Endeavour, owned by Giulio Audisio di Somma.

Holland and Denmark; worth mentioning are the Spicaway imports, among whom are Spicaway Quartz (sire Perrancourt Pirate Prince), Spicaway Son Of A Bitch (sired by Pirate Prince on loan) and Spicaway Margi (sired by Ballintober Envoy For Jokyl).

At the Ginger kennels, owned by Alessandra Picenardi, Ginger The Godfather (sire Spicaway Ouzo) has been used at stud and a Finnish bitch, Big Lady's Unicorn (sire Jokyl Lucky Strike) has been imported.

JAPAN
By Takemi Sugimoto, translation by Kumi Ishihara

Colonel Soichi Imanda first introduced the Airedale to Japan. He wrote two books about the breed, one in 1931 and a second in 1937. He was a true Airedale man who felt the dog was an all-rounder with character.

In 1932, the Imperial Military Dog Association was formed and the dogs chosen were Airedales, German Shepherd Dogs and Dobermanns, for their military usefulness.

Rising von Rokki Chanary's Line, owned by Y. Nomura.

Cedar Creeks Queenbe, owned by C. Kimura, bred by I. Sugiura.

Airedales were considered clever dogs and peaceful by nature and, in 1947, started to be used by the Japan Police Dog Association. The Airedale Terrier Club supplies dogs recognised for their police work, and sometimes these police Airedales win top honours in the show ring.

The Airedale Terrier Club of Japan was formed in 1998. At the first show (April 1998), the BoB was Rising Von Chanarys Line (Jin Von Rokko Canarys Line x Saredon Emerald City), breeder/owner Mr Yukinobu Nomura. BoS – Cedar Creeks Queenbee (Eng. Ch. Saredon Start The Fire x Cedar Creeks Glamorchan), breeder Mr I. Sugiura, owner Mrs Chikako Kimura.

At the autumn show, BoB – Rising von Rokko Chanrys Line. BoS – Camargue of Wilderness (Saredon El Gallo x Barcelona Bloom of Wilderness), breeder Mr T. Sugimoto, owner Mitsuyo Matsubara. At the first Championship show, in April 1999, Rising von Rokko Chanrys won his title.

AUSTRALIA
by Sue Henderson

Aust. Ch. Stanstead That'll Do For Jokyl (Imp. UK) (Ch. Jokyl Lucky Strike x Stanstead That'll Do Nicely), known as

Bennett, was selected by Peter and Jan Hatton while on a trip to the UK. He was purchased in partnership with Sue and Lindsay Henderson and Pauline Lewis and arrived in Melbourne in 1996. At this time, there was a great need for some new blood into the Airedale terrier gene pool in Australia. There had been very few imports for several years and no males from the UK since the early 1980s.

Bennett's show campaign commenced in April 1997 and at his first show he was awarded Runner-up in Group under a terrier specialist. He was only shown lightly through the year and won BIS All Breeds, Runner-up in Show all-breeds, and BIS at the Airedale Terrier Club of Victoria's Championship show. Two of these wins were under Airedale Terrier specialists. He also won Airedale Terrier Club of Victoria's award for the most successful exhibit at Metropolitan shows continuing that year to win four BIG and several Runner-up In Group awards.

During 1998 he was campaigned for only six months and he still clearly won two of the most prestigious awards for an Airedale: Top Victorian Airedale of the year and also Breed Representative and Finalist at the Top Terrier Extravaganza. He was also the winner of the Sires' Produce Stakes at the ATCV's Championship show.

Gisela Lesh owns the famous Strongfort kennels in New South Wales. Probably her best known Airedale is Aust. Grand Ch. Strongfort Solaris (B) (Aust. Ch. & Am. Ch. Cripple Creek Great Gatsby (imp. USA) x Aust. Ch. Strongfort Showise), call name 'Big Bertha'. To date, she is still 'the first and only' Airedale Terrier Grand Champion, winning six BIS, seven Runner-up to BIS, and 32 BIG. Her sire, Aust. Ch. & Am. Ch. Cripple Creek Great Gatsby (Imp. USA) (Am. Ch. Tartan Texas Ranger x Am. Ch. Westmoors Sabella) won seven BIS, five Runner-up to BIS and 26 BIG. Aust. Ch. Strongfort Sexpot (B) (Aust. Ch. Bengal Valley Forge x Aust. Ch. Kiamaire Yarra Lass) was Terrier of the Year 1974-75. Three times BIS at the British Terrier Club Championship Show, she took 11 BIS and was Runner-up to BIS four times.

Among the imported dogs, the bitch Aust. Ch. Rotmon Natascha Bright (imp. Rus.) (Int. Ch. Perrancourt Pirate Prince (UK) x Rus. Ch. Desdemona Von Rottumer Hof (Germ.)) won four BIS, one Runner-up to BIS and seven BIG. Aust. Ch. Iiurrant Hi Flyer (imp. UK) (D) (Ginger Voila of Stanstead (UK) x Aust. Ch. Calamity Jane At Iiurrant (imp. UK), call name 'Ben', was only shown eight times and won four BIG, four Runner-up to BIG and one BIS. All her Airedales are owned/handled/prepared by Gisela.

Rebecca and Russell Harvey (Fyreoayre), NSW, have been involved in Airedales for ten years, have bred five litters and produced five champions: Ch. Bajan Voodoo Dreamer CD, Ch. Rangeaire Royal Princess, Ch. Fyreoayre Royal Prince, Ch. Southdale Black Magic and Ch. Fyreoayre Black Lace.

Sue Jolly (Lachindale) has Ch. Lufttal Laird O'Lufttal. 'Murphy' gained his Championship title by the age of twelve months, and was winner of the Lufttal trophy (Runner-up to Top Challenge Winning Airedale for 1991-92 for the ATA of NSW) amongst other awards.

ARGENTINA
By Julio Maria De Cristofaro

When in our country, Argentina, we speak

Aust. Ch. Stanstead That'll Do For Jokyl (imp. UK), owned by Hatton, Henderson and Lewis.

of Airedales, we think of England at once. Strong bonds tie us with that country. Since last century, these bonds became even closer, evident in the development of culture, public transport, railroad business, and general trade companies. This has led to English families settling in Argentina. They brought the first Airedales with them, and gave us the opportunity to get to know our beloved breed.

For the purpose of this article, I will start with 1960. In this decade, a lot of studs and bitches came from England including Ch. Bengal Carnival, Ch. Bengal Squire, Ch. Bengal Knight, among some others. They improved the overall quality of the existing Airedales.

At the beginning of the seventies, German bloodlines came to our country: vigour and stamina were the slogan; this important part of the history we owe to Ch. Graf von der Canisburg. With him came Vivian von der Canisburg, and from England Ch. Siccawei Penny Royal.

In the mid-seventies, Ch. Wait 'N' See of Joykl was imported form England to Villa Gesell, a beautiful beach town on the Atlantic Ocean, 400 km south-west from Buenos Aires. He imprinted lots of class on his offspring. With him came the best bitch ever to be imported from England – Ch. Hillcross Heidee.

In the late seventies, Ch. Bengal Tarquin arrived. He imprinted class, great quality and most of all his air. With him, the Airedale Terrier was at the top of the Ranking of the Federacion Cinologica Argentina. For the first time in history, an Airedale was third best dog of all breeds. He came accompanied by Bengal Sapphire.

In the eighties, from Brazil came Ch. Bengal Bay Gordon's Pomp and Circumstance, he had lots of beautiful offspring. Ch. Perrancourt Piquet also arrived at this time and was highly influential at stud.

In the late eighties, Ch. Black Jack Ring Star was imported from the United States. With all the important breeding that had been done with English bloodlines, this new American dog stamped on his offspring the great qualities of his father, Ch. Black Jack Mighty Samson. He was mostly responsible for improving hind movement.

At the beginning of the nineties, we had Ch. Bravo Ironman Of Santeric on leave from the United States for a year. Some years later, Ch. Black Jack's Danny Double arrived.

A product of the importations of different quality bloodlines and the hard work and effort of Airedale breeder, the first English Champion born in Argentina crystalised – Ch. Fenomeno de Nagual, bred by Alsina.

This is a short history of our great dogs. We managed to combine the important English influence in our dogs' bloodlines with German and American bloodlines. Now, we are working together to continue to improve the quality of the Airedale Terrier in Argentina.